eBay Commerce Cookbook

Chuck Hudson

O'REILLY®

Beijing · Cambridge · Farnham · Köln · Sebastopol · Tokyo

eBay Commerce Cookbook

by Chuck Hudson

Published by O'Reilly Media, Inc., 1005 Gravenstein Highway North, Sebastopol, CA 95472.

O'Reilly books may be purchased for educational, business, or sales promotional use. Online editions are also available for most titles (*http://my.safaribooksonline.com*). For more information, contact our corporate/institutional sales department: 800-998-9938 or *corporate@oreilly.com*.

Editor: Mary Treseler
Production Editor: Kara Ebrahim

Copyeditor: Rachel Head
Proofreader: Kara Ebrahim
Cover Designer: Randy Comer
Interior Designer: David Futato
Illustrator: Rebecca Demarest

December 2012:   First Edition

Revision History for the First Edition:

2012-12-20   First release

See *http://oreilly.com/catalog/errata.csp?isbn=9781449320157* for release details.

ISBN: 978-1-449-32015-7

[LSI]

To Michele, Sierra, and Alexandra. Thank you for fueling my creativity, keeping me young, and showing me what is most important: you.

Table of Contents

Preface

How We Do Commerce

The way in which we do commerce across the globe has changed greatly in the last decade, and indeed in just the last couple of years. No longer can commerce be thought of as solely completed in brick-and-mortar storefronts and on PCs, through online commerce sites. We now have commerce anywhere and everywhere, through mobile devices and card readers that plug into our smartphones. Business models have expanded past the "freemium" and premium models used extensively online into innovative concepts such as social commerce and "causium" implementations. The commerce lifecycle is literally changing before our eyes.

On a recent trip to San Francisco, I found myself in one of the on-demand car service options traveling from my hotel across town to the Moscone conference center. While riding along, I realized that I had forgotten to purchase a birthday present for a friend. Using my smartphone, I looked up my friend's wish list on a popular online shopping site and purchased a present to be shipped out that day in a few simple clicks. The site let me sign in quickly via my mobile device, find my friend's wish list, see what was recommended for her, and check out without even having to pull out my credit card. I then remembered that the night before another friend had paid for dinner and I wanted to reimburse him for my half. So I opened my PayPal app on the phone and quickly transferred some funds to him.

In that short ride, I had completed multiple commerce transactions. When we arrived at the conference center, I handed my credit card to the driver, who took out his smartphone and plugged in a tiny card reader. He proceeded to swipe my credit card, input the total, and have me sign, and then emailed me a receipt.

The point of this story is that commerce is not only happening anywhere and at any time due to an explosion of smartphone usage, but customers are being introduced to a new level of convenience and features that are quickly becoming the expected level of service. Multiple models support these features, including ecommerce, mobile commerce (mcommerce), and social commerce (scommerce). Who knows what the next "initial-commerce" model will be? eBay has recognized this explosion of new models and established the X.commerce (*http://www.x.com/*) initiative, aimed at supporting the commerce models currently being used and ones yet to be invented. Many of the examples in this text leverage the knowledge and code of the X.com website, and it is a recommended source if you plan to be heavily involved in this area.

Even if you are familiar with the basic use cases of the various eBay APIs, you may not have leveraged any of the many other API sets from other eBay properties to tap into the greater commerce lifecycle. In this book, you will be able explore functional examples that can be applied to generate more demand, traffic, and sales. The examples are designed so that you can jump in feet first and skip the rudimentary details that you may already be familiar with. If you are not familiar with a particular API being used, the example will discuss the basic concepts while providing links to further online documentation and examples. By the end of the book the examples will have covered a wide range of real-life scenarios, showing you how to incorporate into your commerce model features and functionality from APIs including eBay, Hunch, Magento, Milo, PayPal, RedLaser, and ql.io.

The goal of this book is to show how, with a little bit of effort and a wealth of powerful APIs, you can create and enhance your commerce flows. The real-life technical examples cover a range of exciting and innovative uses of the APIs, from generating social recommendations using Twitter feeds to sharing products with friends by scanning QR codes with the RedLaser API. The examples are designed to take you past the basic transaction steps and into functional areas that create a strong commerce lifecycle, combining business strategy with technical solutions.

Creating a Lifecycle

Generally speaking, the focus of any business is to implement an easy-to-use transaction payment system for goods or services so that customers can pay for what they want quickly and efficiently. The premise of this cookbook is that commerce in any form—online, mobile, social, or even storefront—should not just be based on a single event in which a customer purchases an item, but instead should be enveloped in a lifecycle that encompasses the purchase transaction as a single step. The lifecycle starts before a customer ever reaches the point of purchase and can continue long past this event. Like an engine that turns over and over to keep a vehicle moving forward, the lifecycle should not stop after the single stroke of a purchase, but rather should optimally create the opportunity for multiple recurring purchases. As the lifecycle matures, the processes and stages that support the cycle become more robust and easier to accomplish.

Figure P-1 shows a simplified commerce lifecycle, which is the basis for the structure of this book. The commerce lifecycle can be more complex, with more steps and sub-steps, but simplifying the lifecycle allows us to focus on the technology that can enhance these core steps or stages.

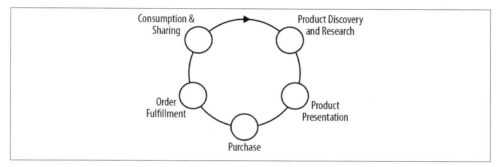

Figure P-1. Simplified commerce lifecycle

The simplified commerce lifecycle is composed of five steps:

1. Product discovery and research
2. Product presentation
3. Purchase through a payment transaction
4. Order fulfillment (shipment and receipt)
5. Consumption and sharing through social commerce

Each step of the simplified lifecycle will be the basis for a chapter of examples in this book. Ultimately, all stages carry equal weight in their opportunity to create long-term customer relationships.

The first stage—product discovery—represents the time and effort that the customer puts into researching, discovering, and identifying a particular offering. Many different sources of knowledge can contribute to this discovery: the user may look at recommendations of similar items, check out local sources of products, or read product reviews. The goal of this stage is to provide the information and data necessary for the user to hone in on a product that she may have sought outright or discovered accidentally.

After the identification of the product in the product discovery stage, the customer moves into a viewing and confirmation stage, labeled here as "product presentation." The product presentation stage provides the user with all the information and data she may need to make that purchase decision, whether by adding the item to a shopping cart or signing up for the service. In either case, as the merchant, you need to provide access to the data and information about the product that the user may seek to trigger the decision to move to the purchase stage. This could include price comparisons, detailed specifications, or other customers' reviews.

The purchase stage is the one that most merchants focus on, since at this stage the customer has decided to make a purchase and proceeds to check out. However, as with the other stages, there are additional features and experiences beyond just the process of entering payment information that can make this stage less complex for the customer. This stage can even be turned into a potentially rewarding process for both the customer and the merchant, through couponing, seamless payments, and opportunities to give to causes. This may increase the likelihood of the customer returning to make more purchases and referring new customers.

After the purchase transaction, the lifecycle continues through order fulfillment and, following this, the customer's use of the good or service purchased. These two stages are often something of an afterthought, due to other efforts being deemed higher priority. However, they can in fact have the greatest impact on whether a customer recommends the product or service and, more importantly, whether he returns to the merchant for future purchases.

The order fulfillment stage represents the period of time after the purchase and until the customer has received the product or service. Timely delivery and communication are essential to passing through this stage smoothly. The last stage—consumption and sharing—is when customers make their final decisions about their commerce experience, formulate opinions of the product or service purchased, and in turn share these opinions—good or bad—throughout their social networks. At the conclusion of this stage, the cycle should not end; instead, if handled well, this stage can feed into the beginning of new cycles with the same customers or contacts in their social networks. The goal is to keep the cycle going and increase the merchant's customer base and sales.

Audience

We can compare the simplified lifecycle of commerce with a standard software development process, as seen in the inner circle of Figure P-1. And just as the simplified lifecycle of commerce works to have multiple revolutions, the software development lifecycle continually improves the resulting products through multiple revolutions. The examples in this book will cover each of these stages, with best practices and notes included with the working technical components.

The book is designed for you, the developer who may have developed ecommerce storefronts, but is looking to or has been tasked with differentiating the business with additional functionality. This differentiation could take the form of incorporating additional features or simplifying procedural steps. A solid programming foundation will be required to implement these examples and apply them to your individual needs. The book assumes you have a hands-on understanding of PHP, HTML, CSS, and JavaScript. While you may not have specific experience with the APIs employed here, the examples are detailed enough to get you started. And even if you are an experienced developer who uses these APIs daily, these examples will hopefully give you some insight into other possible ways to employ the API set, or one of the many other APIs from the other sites referenced in the book.

There are three things working against creating this type of cookbook of commerce examples. First, the examples shown here attempt to meet specific needs, and it has been arduous to pick those examples that will be the most impactful to the most people. Secondly, while we will cover a wide array of eBay-owned APIs, it would be impossible to cover the API set in its entirety in this short text. Lastly, the APIs can of course be integrated into a wide set of technologies, and I only have room to show one implementation. So in the end, this is just a sampling of APIs that can be employed and applied to the stages of the simplified commerce lifecycle. The goal of the solutions picked for inclusion here is to provide an introduction to the wide set of APIs that are part of the eBay properties available, while touching on some of the more directly applicable examples of enhancing the commerce lifecycle in all its stages.

For your specific solution you may be coding in some other language than that used in these examples, but the logic flow for each example should be fairly similar. The examples included here are meant to drive creativity and provide examples on which to base your own solutions. The code examples are exactly that, examples, and are not necessarily meant to be drop-in production-quality code. You will want to add in your own level of deeper error handling and integration. An effort has been made to point out in the examples where these handlers and modularization would be important. Ultimately, the goal is to provide individual examples that can be independently applied to a wide variety of solutions for you, the commerce developer.

How This Book Is Organized

The book consists of five chapters following the simplified commerce lifecycle:

- Chapter 1 provides examples covering the mapping of product availability to location using Milo, listing your products on eBay, and incorporating product reviews from eBay into your site.
- Chapter 2 provides examples including customizing the Magento storefront, personalizing a store experience with PayPal Access, and presenting similar items from eBay.
- Chapter 3 provides examples including autogenerating coupons with Magento, payment preapproval, and donating on checkout with PayPal Adaptive Payments.

- Chapter 4 provides examples covering shipping form creation with PayPal Instant Payment Notifications, shipping method extensions with Magento, and multiple supplier payment with PayPal chained payments.
- Chapter 5 includes examples on facilitating social recommendations with QR codes, generating taste graphs and recommendations via Hunch, and social sharing using mashups through ql.io.

One can write about the steps needed to enhance a specific commerce flow, but there is nothing like doing it firsthand. This book is laid out with working examples (three per chapter) that can be taken in part or as a whole and applied to a business built on commerce flows. Each example is built to take advantage of one or more sets of readily available APIs from one of the multiple eBay-owned businesses.

There is a description of an opportunity that the example is driving to take advantage of and a high-level view of a possible solution at the beginning of each example. Then the example dives into a step-by-step implementation of the solution. While the examples in this book provide each step needed to complete a working project with the specific APIs, the goal is also to empower you with knowledge of how the APIs work, and most importantly, how to work with the APIs outside of the confines of these examples. Thus, you will not only have the benefit of seeing how to use the specific examples in your website or application, but you will also gain knowledge about these APIs for your toolbox going forward.

In the step-by-step directions, I have tried to also focus on providing tips and tricks for integrating the code into your own site and troubleshooting when things do not go so smoothly. Knowing how to troubleshoot the issues can be critical—whether because of configuration differences or just the intricacies of trying to modify the examples to fit your needs, it's inevitable that something will not work.

To try and reach the broadest audience, the examples use some of the more standard web technologies, including PHP, JavaScript, HTML, and CSS. Where possible, the examples use the latest implementations of the technologies, such as various HTML5 and CSS3 features, while at the same time trying to stay clear of technologies that may not currently be universally supported across browsers.

If the opportunity presents itself, other technologies or libraries used in the industry today (such as JQuery) are brought in so that you can see various methods of implementation. When applicable in the examples, notes, recommendations, and best practices are also inserted to save you time and expedite integration of the APIs. At the end of each example a section titled "See Also" is appended, with links to various supporting information and material for working with the APIs used in the example. This section is not meant as an exhaustive list of resources, but rather as a reference to the key areas where you can find more information for your specific implementation.

Differentiating Your Offering

The expectations of customers are changing by the minute, and technologies are allowing for great new commerce delivery methods. It is difficult enough to build your business and keep up with these demands, without even considering trying to differentiate your offering.

This is where external APIs come into play and can be extremely helpful. There are numerous methods available to enhance the lifecycle described earlier by creating stronger relationships, increasing the number of prospective sales that are completed, and encouraging customers to return. Building these features into your solution from scratch can be prohibitive from both a cost and a timing perspective, but through the use of external APIs you can leverage the work of others and integrate the knowledge, information, and data held in systems throughout the Web into your own. Doing so gives you the opportunity to increase the numbers of consumers that successfully complete cycles and to differentiate your offering along the way.

Some of the more prominent questions that you may have asked already to fuel your own commerce cycle include:

- How do I make my products or services visible to targeted consumers?
- How can I leverage social commerce efficiently?
- How can viral marketing take off around my offering?

The intention of this book is to get your creative juices flowing and give you ideas that can be applied to answer these types of questions. The book has combined passions of mine, including business commerce strategy and APIs, to solve technical challenges. It is my hope that you find the cookbook beneficial for your projects, whether you're dealing with ecommerce, mcommerce, scommerce, or even the "x-commerce" that has not been created yet.

Conventions Used in This Book

The following typographical conventions are used in this book:

Italic

> Indicates new terms, URLs, email addresses, filenames, file paths, and file extensions

`Constant width`

> Used for program listings and commands to be typed literally by the user, as well as within paragraphs to refer to program elements such as variable or function names, databases, statements, and keywords

Constant width italic

Shows text that should be replaced with user-supplied values or by values determined by context

This icon signifies a tip, suggestion, or general note.

This icon indicates a warning or caution.

This Book's Example Files

You can download all of the code examples for this book from GitHub at the following location:

https://github.com/cahudson/eBayCommerceCookbook

In the example files you will find the completed versions of the applications built in the book, which will contain all the code required to run them. In a few cases you will need to download additional content files, such as SDKs, from their original sites before running the application; consult the *README* file in the top-level folder for details.

Using Code Examples

This book is here to help you get your job done. In general, if this book includes code examples, you may use the code in your programs and documentation. You do not need to contact us for permission unless you're reproducing a significant portion of the code. For example, writing a program that uses several chunks of code from this book does not require permission. Selling or distributing a CD-ROM of examples from O'Reilly books does require permission. Answering a question by citing this book and quoting example code does not require permission. Incorporating a significant amount of example code from this book into your product's documentation does require permission.

We appreciate, but do not require, attribution. An attribution usually includes the title, author, publisher, and ISBN. For example: "*eBay Commerce Cookbook* by Chuck Hudson (O'Reilly). Copyright 2013 Chuck Hudson, 978-1-449-32015-7."

If you feel your use of code examples falls outside fair use or the permission given here, feel free to contact us at *permissions@oreilly.com*.

Safari® Books Online

 Safari Books Online (*www.safaribooksonline.com*) is an on-demand digital library that delivers expert content in both book and video form from the world's leading authors in technology and business.

Technology professionals, software developers, web designers, and business and creative professionals use Safari Books Online as their primary resource for research, problem solving, learning, and certification training.

Safari Books Online offers a range of product mixes and pricing programs for organizations, government agencies, and individuals. Subscribers have access to thousands of books, training videos, and prepublication manuscripts in one fully searchable database from publishers like O'Reilly Media, Prentice Hall Professional, Addison-Wesley Professional, Microsoft Press, Sams, Que, Peachpit Press, Focal Press, Cisco Press, John Wiley & Sons, Syngress, Morgan Kaufmann, IBM Redbooks, Packt, Adobe Press, FT Press, Apress, Manning, New Riders, McGraw-Hill, Jones & Bartlett, Course Technology, and dozens more. For more information about Safari Books Online, please visit us online.

How to Contact Us

Please address comments and questions concerning this book to the publisher:

O'Reilly Media, Inc.
1005 Gravenstein Highway North
Sebastopol, CA 95472
800-998-9938 (in the United States or Canada)
707-829-0515 (international or local)
707-829-0104 (fax)

We have a web page for this book, where we list errata, examples, and any additional information. You can access this page at *http://oreil.ly/ebay-cookbook*.

To comment or ask technical questions about this book, send email to *bookques tions@oreilly.com*.

For more information about our books, courses, conferences, and news, see our website at *http://www.oreilly.com*.

Find us on Facebook: *http://facebook.com/oreilly*

Follow us on Twitter: *http://twitter.com/oreillymedia*

Watch us on YouTube: *http://www.youtube.com/oreillymedia*

Acknowledgments

First, thank you to Mary Treseler, editorial strategist with O'Reilly Media, who from day one has believed in the proposal for this book and supported it through all the stages. Mary, you have been extremely patient as unexpected events throughout the project threw off already tight timelines. With your fortitude for driving projects we now have a text that I can indeed say I am proud of. I thank you for the opportunity.

The effort that goes into creating a book such as this is all-consuming and takes a toll on friendships and family. Thank you to all my friends and family for their understanding while I have disappeared to complete this project. Without your ongoing support I could not have finished it, and I look forward to catching up.

Over the years the people designing, creating, and supporting the APIs discussed in the text have been extremely open with their time and knowledge, helping me solve some challenging problems. Without the team at X.commerce, PayPal, and eBay, who have not only been evangelists for the APIs but also reviewers, editors, and contributors, this book would not have been possible. Special thanks especially to Praveen Alavilli, John Jawed, Jonathan LeBlanc, and Matthew Russell for their endless knowledge sharing, review feedback, and guidance. Their input has greatly strengthened the quality and value of the examples. Thank you also to Carolyn Mellor and Delyn Simons for the many opportunities you have provided to me along the way in the eBay ecosystem. I look forward to our paths crossing on future projects, wherever they may take us.

Lastly, thank you to all the project partners that have provided the opportunity to create solutions to challenging business problems. The lessons learned and knowledge gained over the years in these projects in both a business strategy and a technical sense are the tools by which I have been able to create this work. I look forward to being continually challenged by the multitude of innovative business ideas and to having the opportunity to lead the next set of disruptions.

CHAPTER 1

Product Discovery and Research

One of the most challenging activities for merchants is attracting new customers to their online or retail sites. Large amounts of funding and effort go into various forms of advertising, including banners, search engine keyword ads, and social or direct marketing to capture eyeballs, increase traffic, and optimally create new customer purchases. At the same time, customers have at hand a large quantity of readily accessible information while researching products or services of interest, which may include reviews and social feeds. These are the challenges of the first step of the simplified commerce lifecycle shown in Figure 1-1—product discovery and research—for both merchants and consumers.

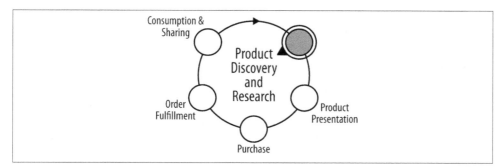

Figure 1-1. Simplified commerce lifecycle—stage 1

In this chapter the examples will focus on leveraging various APIs to connect merchants with potential customers and customers with information to make their research more effective. The first example will cover incorporating eBay user reviews into a site to provide customers with opinions about products they may be contemplating purchasing. The goal is to provide visitors with enough information to make a purchase decision, so they don't need to leave your site in search of more. For those customers that have an immediate need, the next example will show how to incorporate local inventory levels to facilitate a "must have now" type of purchase. The last recipe will look at getting greater exposure of your products by using APIs to list items in the eBay marketplace, where literally thousands of people may discover these products and a merchant's online business.

By incorporating the functionality provided by the APIs shown here, you should be able to minimize the length of time that a potential consumer needs to research a product in this initial stage, and broaden the scope of potential consumers who know of your offering. The aim is to allow more customers to discover your products and to ensure that they have at hand the necessary information to make a buying decision, rather than seeking an alternate source for that information.

1.1. Tapping Into Product Reviews and Guides

Opportunity

For many online and offline customers, purchasing decisions are affected by recommendations from their circles of contacts. These circles may be small (close networks of friends and family) or large (including online reviews from other consumers who may have already purchased the product or had an experience with a site). For the merchant, providing online reviews of products by purchasers is rapidly becoming an expectation, and for consumers, this is becoming a required piece of data for product selection. Fortunately, including consumer reviews with your product information is not as difficult as you might expect, and there are several established repositories of reviews that can be tapped.

Solution

The eBay Shopping developers API provides an API call called `FindReviewsAnd Guides` that opens access to product reviews and buying guides created by eBay users, along with average rating data for any product in the eBay catalog. Passing an internal eBay product ID into the `FindReviewsAndGuides` call can retrieve the applicable reviews. This example will go through a sample flow of finding a product in the catalog that could match one that you provide and then displaying the average rating, the number of reviews, and a list of the most recent reviews.

Discussion

The eBay Shopping API is designed with a series of calls for searching items on eBay. In addition, the API includes calls to retrieve products from a stock catalog that eBay maintains. An overview of the entire eBay Shopping API can be found online in the Shopping API Guide (*http://bit.ly/XFZpzw*).

To retrieve reviews for a product, you first need to know the internal eBay product ID for that specific item. eBay provides a Shopping API call called `FindProducts` to facilitate locating this product ID. A sample `FindProducts` XML request is in Example 1-1; it will perform a search for products that match the query string "Amazon+kindle+fire".

Example 1-1. FindProducts request

```
<?xml version="1.0" encoding="utf-8"?>
<FindProductsRequest xmlns="urn:ebay:apis:eBLBaseComponents">
  QueryKeywords>Amazon+kindle+fire</QueryKeywords>
</FindProductsRequest>
```

This is the most basic use of the `FindProducts` call; other fields exist to limit and filter results by category, pages of results, and sort order. The `QueryKeywords` field has a minimum length of 3 characters and maximum length of 350 characters and allows for the use of wildcard characters (+, −, and *) for further refinement or enlargement of your search. The request will provide an XML response containing all matching products in corresponding product blocks, as seen in the sample response in Example 1-2.

Example 1-2. FindProducts response

```
<?xml version="1.0" encoding="UTF-8"?>
<FindProductsResponse xmlns="urn:ebay:apis:eBLBaseComponents">
  <Timestamp>2012-07-08T13:42:23.164Z</Timestamp>
  <Ack>Success</Ack>
  <Build>E781_CORE_BUNDLED_15030490_R1</Build>
  <Version>781</Version>
  <ApproximatePages>3</ApproximatePages>
  <MoreResults>true</MoreResults>
  <PageNumber>1</PageNumber>
  <Product>
    <DomainName>Tablets</DomainName>
    <DetailsURL>
      http://syicatalogs.ebay.com/ws/
      eBayISAPI.dll?PageSyiProductDetails&amp;IncludeAttributes=
      1&amp;ShowAttributesTable=1&amp;ProductMementoString=
      117984:2:21418:574021108:424383568:730a26cc1986d38949
      d2048fe33ce24e:1:1:1:5000000768188
    </DetailsURL>
    <DisplayStockPhotos>true</DisplayStockPhotos>
    <ProductID type="Reference">110592598</ProductID>
    <ReviewCount>383</ReviewCount>
    <StockPhotoURL>
      http://i.ebayimg.com/00/$(KGrHqR,!jgE5)db1gtTBOmNLBOggw~~_
```

```
    6.JPG?set_id=89040003C1
  </StockPhotoURL>
  <Title>Amazon Kindle Fire 8GB, Wi-Fi, 7in - Black</Title>
</Product>
<Product>
  ...
  ...
<TotalProducts>3</TotalProducts>
</FindProductsResponse>
```

If the search finds more than 2,000 products, the API call will return an error and you should further refine the search.

Most businesses that deal with products will have some code as part of their inventory information that uniquely identifies a particular product, such as a UPC code or an ISBN number. With FindProducts, you can also use one of these unique identifiers to isolate and retrieve the internal eBay product ID. Instead of using the QueryKeywords property, you would use the ProductID property, providing an ID type as an attribute and the ID in the value of the XML node:

```
<ProductID type="ISBN">9780321769381</ProductID>
```

For a list of the product types allowed, see the FindProducts call reference page (*http:// developer.ebay.com/devzone/shopping/docs/CallRef/FindProducts.html*).

So you don't have to program your entire solution to see if the API calls will provide the data you need and to verify that your requests are properly structured, eBay provides an API Test Tool (*https://developer.ebay.com/DevZone/build-test/test-tool/default.aspx*), seen in Figure 1-2, through developer.ebay.com. You can use this tool not only to exercise the Shopping API calls with sample structures of XML requests, but also to exercise other API sets from eBay. The tool will take your request and execute the call selected, providing the response XML block. In this manner you can select and test your call flows prior to full implementation of the solution in code.

To execute any of the Shopping API calls, you will need to register with the eBay developer network (*https://developer.ebay.com/*) and go to the My Account section to create and retrieve your application key sets. An application key set can be generated for a testing sandbox (*http://sandbox.ebay.com*) and for the production environment. The application key set will contain three IDs that are sent with your API request:

- *DevID*
- *AppID*
- *CertID*

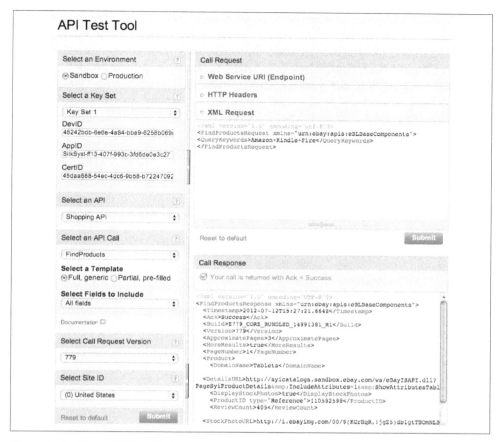

Figure 1-2. eBay API Test Tool

The AppID will be needed for the calls in this example, and a different set will need to be used based on whether you are making sandbox or production requests. When you have your application key sets, you can use the API Test Tool under Development Tools to validate the credentials. An easy test call to make is `GeteBayTime`, under the Shopping API. The call has a simple request format with no arguments passed in the XML block and will return the current eBay time for the site specified on the left side of the tool. The site ID represents the applicable eBay country site; for these examples, 0 will be used for the site ID, which corresponds to the United States.

The eBay Shopping API has a request limit of 5,000 queries per day, per IP address. If you need a higher limit, you can apply for an increase by having your application certified through the Compatible Application Check program (*http://bit.ly/R3LFAg*).

The first web page of our example will allow the user to enter a keyword or keywords to search for, in a form. The form will be posted to the same page and the FindProd ucts API call will be constructed and sent to the eBay API servers via a PHP curl command. The XML response block will then be parsed by looping through each product in the response, and the product name, image, and product ID for each will be retrieved. Each product will be displayed and linked to a second page, passing the product ID when selected. Example 1-3 has the code for the *findProducts.php* page.

Example 1-3. findProducts.php

```php
<?php
/*********************************************
findProducts.php

Uses FindProducts to retrieve list of
products based on keyword query.

*********************************************/

// include our Shopping API constants
require_once 'shoppingConstants.php';

// check if posted
if (!empty($_POST)) {

  // grab our posted keywords and call helper function
  $query = $_POST['query'];
  $response = getFindProducts($query);

  // create a simple XML object from results
  $xmlResponse = simplexml_load_string($response);
}

// function to call the Shopping API FindProducts
function getFindProducts($query) {

  // create the XML request
  $xmlRequest  = "<?xml version=\"1.0\" encoding=\"utf-8\"?>";
  $xmlRequest .= "<FindProductsRequest
    xmlns=\"urn:ebay:apis:eBLBaseComponents\">";
  $xmlRequest .= "<QueryKeywords>" . $query . "</QueryKeywords>";
  $xmlRequest .= "<ProductSort>Popularity</ProductSort>";
  $xmlRequest .= "<SortOrder>Descending</SortOrder>";
  $xmlRequest .= "<MaxEntries>100</MaxEntries>";
  $xmlRequest .= "<HideDuplicateItems>true</HideDuplicateItems>";
  $xmlRequest .= "</FindProductsRequest>";

  // define our header array for the Shopping API call
  $headers = array(
    'X-EBAY-API-APP-ID:'.API_KEY,
    'X-EBAY-API-VERSION:'.SHOPPING_API_VERSION,
```

```
   'X-EBAY-API-SITE-ID:'.SITE_ID,
   'X-EBAY-API-CALL-NAME:FindProducts',
   'X-EBAY-API-REQUEST-ENCODING:'.RESPONSE_ENCODING,
   'Content-Type: text/xml;charset=utf-8'
 );

 // initialize our curl session
 $session  = curl_init(SHOPPING_API_ENDPOINT);

 // set our curl options with the XML request
 curl_setopt($session, CURLOPT_HTTPHEADER, $headers);
 curl_setopt($session, CURLOPT_POST, true);
 curl_setopt($session, CURLOPT_POSTFIELDS, $xmlRequest);
 curl_setopt($session, CURLOPT_RETURNTRANSFER, true);

 // execute the curl request
 $responseXML = curl_exec($session);

 // close the curl session
 curl_close($session);

 // return the response XML
 return $responseXML;
}
?>

<!DOCTYPE html>
<html>
<head>
<meta charset="UTF-8" />
<title>1-2 Find Products with FindProducts</title>
<style>
body {background: #fff; color: #000;
  font: normal 62.5%/1.5 tahoma, verdana, sans-serif;}
* {margin: 0; padding: 0;}
form {padding: 0 10px; width: 700px;}
legend {font-size: 2em; padding-left: 5px; padding-right: 5px;
  position: relative;}
fieldset {border: 1px solid #ccc; border-radius: 5px; padding: 10px;
  width: 320px;}
li {clear: both; list-style-type: none; margin: 0 0 10px;}
label, input {font-size: 1.3em;}
label {display: block; padding: 0 0 5px; width: 200px;}
input {background-position: 295px 5px; background-repeat: no-repeat;
  border: 2px solid #ccc; border-radius: 5px;
  padding: 5px 25px 5px 5px; width: 285px;}
input:focus {outline: none;}
input:invalid:required {background-image: url(asterisk.png);
  box-shadow: none;}
input:focus:invalid {background-image: url(invalid.png);
  box-shadow: 0px 0px 5px #b01212; border: 2px solid #b01212;}
input:valid:required {background-image: url(accept.png);
  border: 2px solid #7ab526;}
```

```
div label {width: 100%;}
div.product {float: left; border: 7px solid #ccc; border-radius: 5px;
  padding: 10px; margin: 10px; height: 150px; width: 200px;
  text-align: center; vertical-align: top;}
div.product:hover {background-color: #39F; border-color: #FF6;}
</style>
</head>
<body>
<div id="frmProduct">
  <!-- simple form for query keyword entry -->
  <form name="search" action="findProducts.php" method="post">
    <fieldset>
      <legend>Product Search</legend>
      <ol>
        <li>
          <label for="query">Keyword</label>
          <input autofocus required id="query" name="query"
            placeholder="Nook" />
        </li>
      </ol>
      <input type="submit" value="Search">
    </fieldset>
    <br/>
  </form>
</div>
<div id="container">

  <?php
    // result block creation if results from form being posted
    // check for valid XML response object
    if ($xmlResponse) {

      echo '<H1>Results for "' . $query . '". Select one.</H1>';

      // loop through each XML product node in the response
      foreach ($xmlResponse->Product as $product) {

        // display the image and title for each product
        // create link to reviews page with internal ProductID
        echo '<a href="showReviews.php?pid=' .
          $product->ProductID . '">';
        echo '<div class="product">';
        if (($product->DisplayStockPhotos)=='true') {
          echo '<img src="' . $product->StockPhotoURL . '" />';
        } else {
          echo '<img src="missing.png" style="height:70px;" />';
        }
        echo "<br/>";
        echo $product->Title;
        echo '</div></a>';
      }
    }
    else {
```

```
      // display message if no search results (not posted)
      echo "Enter a search keyword above.";
    }
  ?>

</div>
</body>
</html>
```

This example uses multiple API calls across pages, so the constants for the credentials have been placed in a separate file, *shoppingConstants.php*. These constants include the API key, URL endpoint, version number of the API being called, eBay site ID, and response encoding type, as seen in Example 1-4. You will need to replace the API key field in the *shoppingConstants.php* file with your AppID. The constants will be used in the headers of the `curl` request on the *findProducts.php* and review retrieval pages.

Example 1-4. shoppingConstants.php

```php
<?php
/*******************************************
shoppingConstants.php

Constants used for Shopping API calls.

*******************************************/

// eBay developer API key
DEFINE("API_KEY","<YOUR_API_KEY>");

// eBay Shopping API constants
DEFINE("SHOPPING_API_ENDPOINT","http://open.api.ebay.com/shopping");
DEFINE("SHOPPING_API_VERSION",779);

// eBay site to use - 0 = United States
DEFINE("SITE_ID",0);

// response encoding format - XML
DEFINE("RESPONSE_ENCODING","XML");
?>
```

After placing the *findProducts.php* and *shoppingConstants.php* pages on your site and browsing to the *findProducts.php* page, type in a keyword to search for and submit the form. If the call is successful, you should see a chart of products, as displayed in Figure 1-3.

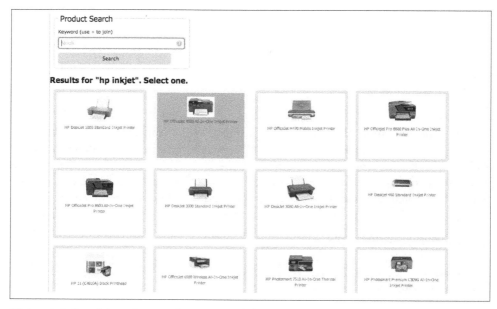

Figure 1-3. Resulting eBay product ID availability map

Now that the product IDs for each product have been retrieved, the reviews retrieval page needs to be added so that when a product is selected, the reviews and ratings for that product can be displayed.

Remember that if you have the ISBN, EAN, or UPC code, you can skip the product search step and make the FindProducts call behind the scenes so that the reviews can be shown directly with the particular product. The keyword search form is used for the sample purpose of making the FindProducts API call.

The reviews retrieval page follows a similar flow to the *findProducts.php* page. Instead of a form, however, the *showReviews.php* page will take a product ID passed in the query string to create an XML request, as seen in Example 1-5, for the eBay Shopping API.

Example 1-5. FindReviewsAndGuides request

```
<?xml version="1.0" encoding="utf-8"?>
<FindReviewsAndGuidesRequest xmlns="urn:ebay:apis:eBLBaseComponents">
  <ProductID type="Reference">110592598</ProductID>
</FindReviewsAndGuidesRequest>
```

The resulting return XML block will contain summary items including the average rating and number of reviews available for the product, followed by the most current reviews in one or more <Review> XML blocks, as seen in Example 1-6.

Example 1-6. FindReviewsAndGuides response

```xml
<?xml version="1.0" encoding="UTF-8"?>
<FindReviewsAndGuidesResponsexmlns="urn:ebay:apis:eBLBaseComponents">
  <Timestamp>2012-07-08T13:45:31.555Z</Timestamp>
  <Ack>Success</Ack>
  <Build>E781_CORE_BUNDLED_15030490_R1</Build>
  <Version>781</Version>
  <ReviewCount>383</ReviewCount>
  <BuyingGuideCount>0</BuyingGuideCount>
  <ProductID type="Reference">110592598</ProductID>
  <ReviewsAndGuidesURL>
    http://search.reviews.ebay.com/
    Amazon-Kindle-Fire-8GB-Wi-Fi-7in-Black?fvcs=5918&amp;sopr=
    110592598&amp;upvr=2
  </ReviewsAndGuidesURL>
  <PageNumber>1</PageNumber>
  <TotalPages>77</TotalPages>
  <BuyingGuideDetails>
    <BuyingGuideHub>
      http://search.reviews.ebay.com/?satitle=
      Amazon+Kindle+Fire+8GB%2C+Wi-Fi%2C+7in+-+Black&amp;uqt=g
    </BuyingGuideHub>
  </BuyingGuideDetails>
  <ReviewDetails>
    <AverageRating>4.5</AverageRating>
    <Review>
      <URL>
        http://search.reviews.ebay.com/
        Amazon-Kindle-Fire-8GB-Wi-Fi-7in-Black?fvcs=5918&amp;sopr=
        110592598&amp;upvr=2
      </URL>
      <Title>
        Fair price should be $199. Just don't expect too m...
      </Title>
      <Rating>4</Rating>
      <Text>
        Kindle Fire is great
        ...
        ...
      </Text>
      <UserID>nopink2000</UserID>
      <CreationTime>2012-03-10T17:16:41.000Z</CreationTime>
    </Review>
    <Review>
      <URL>
        http://search.reviews.ebay.com/
        Amazon-Kindle-Fire-8GB-Wi-Fi-7in-Black?fvcs=5918&amp;sopr=
```

```
      110592598&amp;upvr=2
  </URL>
  <Title>Excellent buy.</Title>
  <Rating>5</Rating>
  <Text>
    I love my Kindle!
    ...
    ...
```

The *showReviews.php* page in Example 1-7 will display the summary product rating information and loop through the reviews, displaying the title, rating, author's eBay username, and text of each review.

Example 1-7. showReviews.php

```php
<?php
/*********************************************
showReviews.php

Uses FindReviewsAndGuides to retrieve list of
most recent reviews.

Called by findProducts.php with ProductID.
*********************************************/

// include our Shopping API constants
require_once 'shoppingConstants.php';

// check if called with query string
if (!empty($_GET)) {

  // get the product ID and call the helper function
  $pid = $_GET['pid'];
  $response = getFindReviewsAndGuides($pid);

  // create a simple XML object from results
  $xmlResponse = simplexml_load_string($response);
}

// function to call the Shopping API FindReviewsAndGuides
function getFindReviewsAndGuides($pid) {

  // create the XML request
  $xmlRequest  = "<?xml version=\"1.0\" encoding=\"utf-8\"?>";
  $xmlRequest .= "<FindReviewsAndGuidesRequest
    xmlns=\"urn:ebay:apis:eBLBaseComponents\">";
  $xmlRequest .= "<ProductID type=\"Reference\">" . $pid .
    "</ProductID>";
  $xmlRequest .= "</FindReviewsAndGuidesRequest>";

  // define our header array for the Shopping API call
  $headers = array(
```

```php
    'X-EBAY-API-APP-ID:'.API_KEY,
    'X-EBAY-API-VERSION:'.SHOPPING_API_VERSION,
    'X-EBAY-API-SITE-ID:'.SITE_ID,
    'X-EBAY-API-CALL-NAME:FindReviewsAndGuides',
    'X-EBAY-API-REQUEST-ENCODING:'.RESPONSE_ENCODING,
    'Content-Type: text/xml;charset=utf-8'
  );

  // initialize our curl session
  $session  = curl_init(SHOPPING_API_ENDPOINT);

  // set our curl options with the XML request
  curl_setopt($session, CURLOPT_HTTPHEADER, $headers);
  curl_setopt($session, CURLOPT_POST, true);
  curl_setopt($session, CURLOPT_POSTFIELDS, $xmlRequest);
  curl_setopt($session, CURLOPT_RETURNTRANSFER, true);

  // execute the curl request
  $responseXML = curl_exec($session);

  // close the curl session
  curl_close($session);

  // return the response XML
  return $responseXML;
}
?>

<!DOCTYPE html>
<html>
<head>
<meta charset="UTF-8" />
<title>1-2 Show Reviews with FindReviewsAndGuides</title>
<style>
body {background: #fff; color: #000;
  font: normal 62.5%/1.5 tahoma, verdana, sans-serif;}
* {margin: 0; padding: 0;}
div#stats {font-size: 1.3em; font-weight: bold; margin: 10px;
  padding: 10px;}
div.reviewHeader {font-size: 1.3em; font-weight: bold;
  border: 7px solid #ccc; border-radius: 5px;
  padding: 10px 10px 20px 10px; margin: −17px 0px 10px −17px;
  width: 500px; vertical-align: top; background-color: #9FC}
div.review {border: 7px solid #ccc; border-radius: 5px; padding: 10px;
  margin: 10px; width: 500px; vertical-align: top;}
</style>
</head>
<body>
<div>
  <a href="findProducts.php">< Back</a>
</div>
<div>
```

```php
<?php
  // Result block creation if results from product ID
  // Check for valid XML response object
  if ($xmlResponse) {

      // display review count, guide count, and average rating
      echo '<H1>Reviews</H1>';
      echo '<div id="stats">';
      echo $xmlResponse->ReviewCount . ' Reviews<br/>';
      echo $xmlResponse->BuyingGuideCount . ' Guides<br/>';
      echo 'Average rating: ' .
        $xmlResponse->ReviewDetails->AverageRating;
      echo '</div>';

      // loop through each XML review node in the response
      foreach ($xmlResponse->ReviewDetails->Review as $review) {

          // display the title, userid, rating, and text for each
          // review based on internal ProductID
          echo '<div class="review">';
          echo '<div class="reviewHeader">';
          echo '<div>' . $review->Title . '</div>';
          echo '<div style="float:left;">' . $review->UserID . '</div>';
          echo '<div style="float:right;">
            <img src="stars' . $review->Rating . '.png"
              style="height:15px;"/></div>';
          echo '</div>';
          echo '<div style="clear:both;"></div>';
          echo '<div class="reviewText">';
          echo $review->Text;
          echo '</div>';
          echo '</div>';
      }
  }
  else {
      // display message if no reviews returned
      echo "No reviews found.";
  }
?>

</div>
</body>
</html>
```

Figure 1-4 shows the resulting screen for *showReviews.php* after having selected a product on the *findProducts.php* page.

Figure 1-4. eBay reviews for the product

This example has shown how the Shopping API provides an easy method to include social data on products in the form of ratings and reviews for potential customers to research. In addition, this information can be combined with other Shopping API calls to show lists of popular items, allowing visitors to discover new products.

See Also

eBay Developer Network (*http://developer.ebay.com/*)

eBay Shopping API Documentation (*https://www.x.com/developers/ebay/products/shopping-api*)

eBay Shopping API FindProducts call reference (*http://developer.ebay.com/DevZone/shopping/docs/CallRef/FindProducts.html*)

eBay Shopping API FindReviewsAndGuides call reference (*http://developer.ebay.com/DevZone/shopping/docs/CallRef/FindReviewsandGuides.html*)

API Test Tool (*https://developer.ebay.com/DevZone/build-test/test-tool/default.aspx*)

1.2. Mapping Product Availability

Opportunity

One of the challenges of having a business storefront is attracting potential customers to what you carry and your product inventory. This results in a significant line item for marketing in any business budget. The Milo.com website provides visitors a means to search for products within a specific radius of their current location or another specified location. Not only can businesses link into this service and integrate their stores and inventory into the results of Milo.com, but also an API is available for integrating the data into your site for your own business needs.

Solution

In this example, we will go through the Milo Open API and its endpoints, specifically looking at the use of Milo product IDs and the Availability endpoint to access current inventory of an item within a certain radius of a location. This can provide a means to get your goods in front of online buyers, who can discover the availability of the product locally from you. For businesses, this API can also provide critical information for verification of your store's inventory and competitive intelligence about other merchants and their pricing, products, and availability.

Discussion

The Milo Open API is focused on three areas of information: merchant locations, product information, and availability. The API is free to developers and has standard rate limits in place for usage. The default rate limit is 5,000 queries per API key per hour. Businesses or developers who hit the rate limit are encouraged to contact the Milo API group via email explaining their situation for possible rate increases. For more information, see the online Milo Open API documentation (*http://www.x.com/developers/documentation-tools/milo/miloindex*).

A per-domain developer API key is required to make calls to the Milo Open API platform. The key is included with your API requests from your pages to validate the origin of the requests. You can acquire a key by going to the X.com developer's portal (*http://devportal.x.com*). If you do not have an account, you will need to create one. Once logged in, click "Manage Applications." This will bring you to "My Applications." Click the "Register Application" button to add a new application that will use the Milo Open API. A form will be displayed for registering your new application, as seen in Figure 1-5. Fill out the form, making sure to check the Milo offering for the API Scope. This will allow your application to access the Milo Open API from the domain that you specify in the form.

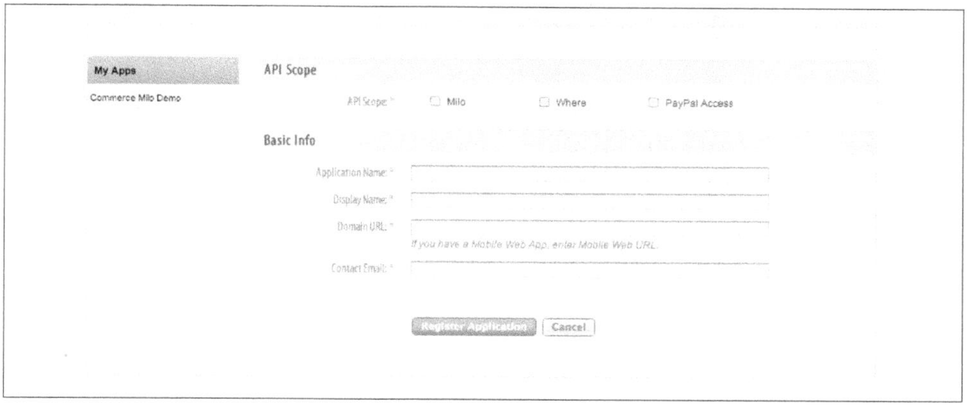

Figure 1-5. X.com new application registration

After submitting the form via the "Register Application" button, you will be provided with your API key, as shown in Figure 1-6. If you forget your API key, you can access it by logging into the developer's portal and viewing your applications. Your API key will be listed with each application you have registered.

Your application "Commerce Milo Demo" has been set up and your API key have been approved.

You are now ready to build applications with this API. We look forward to seeing what you build!

Application Name: Commerce Milo Demo
App ID: 894ca713e08a2a83107be238b2nd6327
App Secret: 1d07a92a2a12f3cf

View Application

Figure 1-6. X.com completed registration for new application

Now that you have an API key, try a call to one of the Milo Open API endpoints to verify that the key works. Open a browser and type in the following URL, replacing *<YOUR_API_KEY>* with the key for your application:

https://api.x.com/milo/v3/store_addresses?key=<YOUR_API_KEY>

If your API key is valid, you will see a list of store addresses returned in JSON format, similar to the one in Figure 1-7.

```
{
   - store_addresses: [
      - {
            phone: "3526742039",
            street: "552 N US Hwy 27",
            postal_code: "32159",
            city: "Lady Lake",
            region: "FL",
            merchant_name: "Best Buy"
         },
      - {

            phone: "6108732312",
            street: "871 E Lancaster Ave",
            postal_code: "19335",
            city: "Downingtown",
            region: "PA",
            merchant_name: "Best Buy"
         },
      - {

            phone: "8138549239",
            street: "11655 W Hillsborough Ave",
            postal_code: "33635",
```

Figure 1-7. Milo store address results from API key test

If your key is invalid, you will get a message saying that you need to register your application here (*http://devportal.x.com*).

 Note that the JSON return in Figure 1-7 and used throughout the book is nicely formatted for visual verification. The formatted output is available via a helpful extension to the Chrome browser called JSONView (*https://chrome.google.com/webstore/detail/chklaanhfefbnpoihckbnef hakgolnmc*).

The test link used to validate your API key is hitting the first of the endpoints of the Milo Open API: the Store Addresses endpoint. This endpoint provides a list of store address blocks of information based on a list of merchant IDs (Milo IDs) or 10-digit phone numbers. The return information can include merchant information, latitude, longitude, hours of operation, and address information for the store.

The second Milo endpoint is the Products endpoint, which will return detailed product data including a list of merchants that carry the product, Milo category IDs, brand IDs, minimum and maximum pricing, image links, and the Milo product ID. Search requests can be performed on keywords or a range of other criteria, including UPC codes. To perform a test search, navigate to this endpoint in your browser with a URL like the one shown here:

https://api.x.com/milo/v3/products?q=nook&key=<YOUR_API_KEY>

Remember to substitute your key for *<YOUR_API_KEY>* and put in an appropriate product keyword for the *q* variable in the query string. To perform a search using a UPC code, use the format *q=upc:<upc_code>*, where the *<upc_code>* field is replaced with a corresponding numerical UPC code. The return for this call should look something like Figure 1-8.

```
{
  - pagination: {
      total_results: 760,
      per_page: 30,
      total_pages: 26,
      page: 0
  },
  - products: [
    - {
        - merchants: [
            1825,
            1779,
            1829
          ],
          min_price: 16900,
          name: "NOOK Color™ by Barnes & Noble",
          max_price: 16999,
          product_id: 6754308
      },
    - {
        - merchants: [
            3040,
            1825,
            1779,
            1829
          ],
          min_price: 9900,
          name: "NOOK The Simple Touch Reader™ by Barnes & Noble",
          max_price: 9999,
          product_id: 9753367
```

Figure 1-8. Return from Products endpoint

The results from the Products endpoint will be paginated and contain a list of matching products and other information. The primary key is the internal Milo product ID, which will be used in the upcoming coding example. If you were presenting a solution to visitors, you would typically show the matching products and have the user select one to see the availability of that product in her area.

The last endpoint, Availability, is how we can access information about the availability of a product at particular stores in a given geographic area. The request takes a specific location, a radius, and a Milo product ID to isolate the local stores carrying that product and the availability levels. The result of the Availability endpoint calls is structured differently from that of the other endpoints, and may be slightly confusing. Unlike the other endpoints, which have a single request/response format, the response for the Availability endpoint returns data via chunked transfer encoding (*http://en.wikipe dia.org/wiki/Chunked_transfer_encoding*). That is, the data is returned in *separate* merchant, store, and inventory response blocks. An inventory block will follow the corresponding store block, which will follow a merchant block. There could be multiple store and inventory blocks for a single merchant, since a merchant could have multiple store locations. The connections of the blocks will be covered more with the web service call in the example.

To map the availability of a particular product (now that we have the Milo product ID from the Products endpoint), open a blank HTML file and paste in the code from Example 1-8.

Example 1-8. productAvail.html product availability map

```
<!DOCTYPE html>
<html>
<head>
<meta charset="UTF-8" />
<title>1-3 Mapping Product Availability with Milo</title>
<script
  src="//ajax.googleapis.com/ajax/libs/jquery/1.7.2/jquery.min.js">
</script>
<style>
body {background: #fff; color: #000;
  font: normal 62.5%/1.5 tahoma, verdana, sans-serif;}
* {margin: 0; padding: 0;}
#container {width: 500px;}
#mapCanvas {width: 500px; height: 300px; border: 1px solid #ccc;
  border-radius: 5px; margin: 22px 10px; padding:10px;}
form {padding: 0 10px; width: 700px;}
legend {font-size: 2em; padding-left: 5px; padding-right: 5px;
  position: relative;}
fieldset {border: 1px solid #ccc; border-radius: 5px; padding: 10px;
  width: 320px;}
li {clear: both; list-style-type: none; margin: 0 0 10px;}
label, input {font-size: 1.3em;}
label {display: block; padding: 0 0 5px; width: 200px;}
input {background-position: 295px 5px; background-repeat: no-repeat;
  border: 2px solid #ccc; border-radius: 5px;
  padding: 5px 25px 5px 5px; width: 285px;}
input:focus {outline: none;}
input:invalid:required {background-image: url(asterisk.png);
  box-shadow: none;}
input:focus:invalid {background-image: url(invalid.png);
  box-shadow: 0px 0px 5px #b01212; border: 2px solid #b01212;}
input:valid:required {background-image: url(accept.png);
  border: 2px solid #7ab526;}
input[type=range]:before{content: "1";}
input[type=range]:after{content: "100";}
div#range label {font-weight: bold;}
output {font-size: 1.3em; font-weight: bold; display: block;
  text-align: center;}
div label {width: 100%;}
```

```
</style>
<script src="http://maps.google.com/maps/api/js?sensor=false"></script>
<script>
// global map reference variable
var map;

// initialize the page
function init() {

  // load and initialize map with default location
  var myLatlng = new google.maps.LatLng(33.85095,-84.2075);
  var myOptions = {
    zoom: 10,
    center: myLatlng,
    mapTypeId: google.maps.MapTypeId.ROADMAP
  }
  map = new google.maps.Map(document.getElementById("mapCanvas"),
    myOptions);


  // add the button click listener
  var btnFindProduct = document.getElementById('findProduct');
  btnFindProduct.addEventListener('click',findProduct,false);

} // end init

// function to call AJAX helper for retrieving availability
function findProduct() {

  // set helper URL location
  var wsUrl = "ajax/wsMiloAvailability.php";

  // grab values from form for product ID search
  var inProduct = document.getElementById('product').value;
  var inZip = document.getElementById('zip').value;
  var inRadius = document.getElementById('radius').value;

  // encapsulate fields for query string
  var params = {
    product_id: inProduct,
    postal_code: inZip,
    radius: inRadius
  };

  // make AJAX call
  $.ajax({ url: wsUrl, data: $.param(params), success: processData});

} // end findProduct

// function to process the availability data received via AJAX
function processData(data) {
```

```
var merName;
var merImg;
var storeLat;
var storeLng;
var storeStock;

// convert JSON data into JSON object
var obj = jQuery.parseJSON(data);

// TODO: should handle if no data or error returned

// loop through each merchant returned
$.each(obj, function(i, merchant) {

    // grab merchant name and image
    merName = this['name'];
    merImg = this['image_url'];

    // loop through each store location of merchant
    $.each(merchant, function() {

        // simple check if a store object
        if (this['id']) {

            // grab the store location information and availability
            storeLat = this['latitude'];
            storeLng = this['longitude'];
            storeStock = this['availability'];

            // create the marker with the data
            createMarker(merName, merImg, storeLat, storeLng, storeStock)
        }
    });
});

// pan to the marker displayed
map.panTo(mkrLatLng);


} // end processData

// function to create each map marker based on passed data
function createMarker(mkrName, mkrImg, mkrLat, mkrLng, mkrStock) {

    /* Milo availbility values include:
        in_stock     Currently available for purchase
        out_of_stock Currently not available for purchase
        limited      Currently available though stock may be low
        carries      The product is sold at the store but availability
                     is unknown
        likely       Likely to be available but not certain
        never        The store does not carry the product
```

```
        call          The store should be contacted for availability
                      information
*/

// check availabilty and set icon to merchant image if available
var mkrIcon = '';
if (mkrStock == 'in_stock' || mkrStock == 'limited') {
  mkrIcon = mkrImg;
}

// create the marker based on Latitude and Longitude
var mkrLatLng = new google.maps.LatLng(mkrLat, mkrLng);
var marker = new google.maps.Marker({
    position: mkrLatLng,
    map: map,
    icon: mkrIcon
});

// set the info window content and click listener to display
var infowindow = new google.maps.InfoWindow();
google.maps.event.addListener(marker, 'click', (function(marker) {
    return function() {
      infowindow.setContent('<img src="' + mkrImg + '" />' + mkrName
        + '<br/>' + mkrStock);
      infowindow.open(map, marker);
    }
})(marker));

} // end createMarker

// initialize the page
window.addEventListener('load',init,false);

</script>
</head>
<body>
<div id="container">
  <div id="mapCanvas"></div>
  <div id="productForm">
    <form>
      <fieldset>
      <legend>Product Search</legend>
      <ol>
        <li>
          <label for="product">Product ID (Milo ID)</label>
          <input autofocus required id="product" name="product"
            value="6754308" />
        </li>
        <li>
          <label for="zip">Zip Code</label>
          <input required id="zip" name="zip" value="30345" />
        </li>
```

```
    <li>
      <label for="radius">Radius (1-100 miles)</label>
      <input required id="radius" name="radius" min="1" max="100"
        value="10" />
    </li>
    </ol>
    </fieldset>
    <br/>
    <button id="findProduct" name="findProduct" type="button">
      Locate Product
    </button>
    </form>
  </div>
</div>
</body>
</html>
```

This page will allow the user to enter a product ID, zip code, and radius in a form. The radius parameter is a range for the search, between 1 and 100 miles. After submitting the form, the page will make a request to a helper web service we will create, which will in turn call the Milo Availability endpoint, get the results, merge them into a single JSON block, and return the block to the HTML page. Once received, the page will map the locations on an embedded Google map, as seen in Figure 1-9. If a store has stock, the page will show the store logo image as the marker. If there is no stock, the marker will be a regular map marker. If you click on the marker, an info window will appear with the merchant logo and a stock count. You could add the store hours, address, and other information from the results as desired.

To assist with the chunked data that is returned from the Availability call, a PHP helper web service has been implemented in this example. The PHP file takes the parameters set in the page, adds them to a request to the Availability endpoint, and executes the call, as if a file were being opened via a URL so that the return can be handled as a stream. Each chunk of data received is a block or line, which is then handled according to the type of data in the block: merchant, location, or availability. The blocks are added as arrays into a master array, which is then encoded in JSON and returned to the HTML page. The code for the PHP web service helper is in Example 1-9.

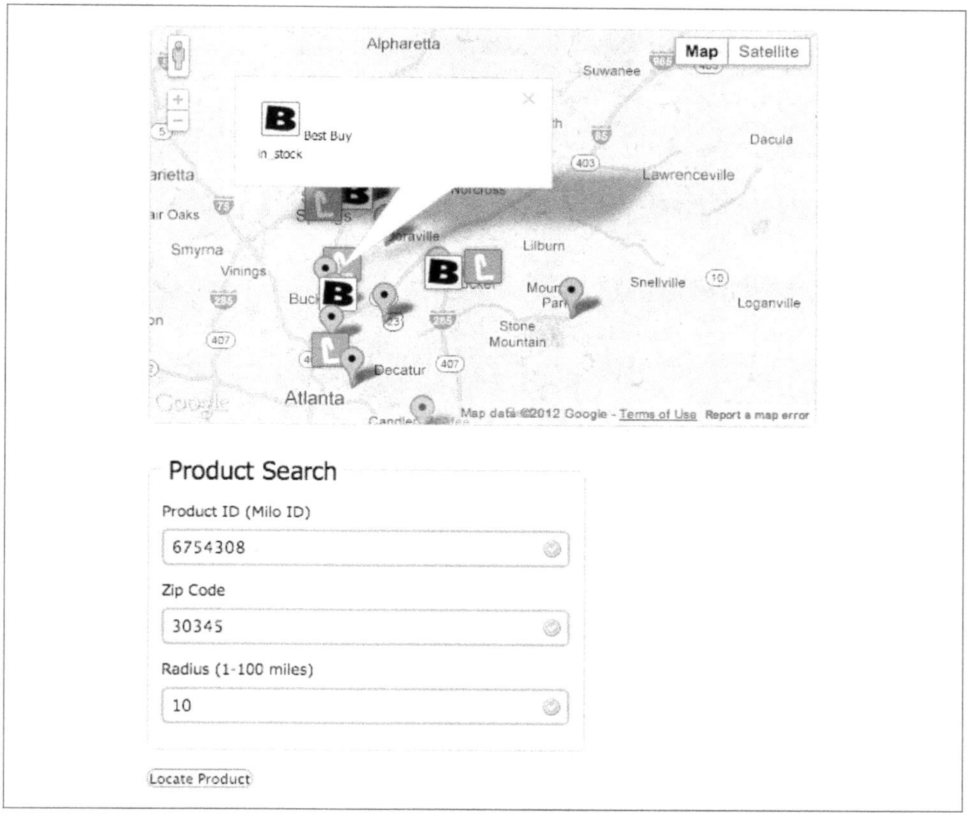

Figure 1-9. Resulting product ID availability map

Example 1-9. wsMiloAvailability.php web service helper

```php
<?php

/*********************************************
wsMiloAvailability.php
Web service helper for accessing Milo Open
API Availabilty endpoint.

API key required for your domain.
Calls  caller.php and APIError.php.
*********************************************/

DEFINE("API_KEY","<YOUR_API_KEY>");
DEFINE("AVAIL_ENDPOINT","https://api.x.com/milo/v3/availability");

// set the URL to call
$url = AVAIL_ENDPOINT . "?key=" . API_KEY . "&" .
  $_SERVER['QUERY_STRING'];
```

```php
// Use a file stream to handle availability chunking of the
// return information. We will loop through all the chunks
// received and collapse to one JSON block.
$file_handle = fopen($url, "r");
if ($file_handle) {

  // array to hold new block for client
  $arr_json = array();

  while (!feof($file_handle)) {

    // get the next line from the file stream
    $line = fgets($file_handle);

    // decode the chunk or line we just received
    $jsonLine = json_decode($line, true);

    // determine chunk type and handle
    switch (key($jsonLine)) {

      // received a merchant chunk
      case "merchant":
        // get the merchant and hold the merchant JSON
        $merchant_id = (string)$jsonLine['merchant']['id'];
        $arr_json[$merchant_id] = $jsonLine["merchant"];
        break;

      // received a store location chunk
      case "location":
        // get the location and add under merchant
        $location_id = (string)$jsonLine['location']['id'];
        $merchant_id = (string)$jsonLine['location']['merchant_id'];
        $arr_json[$merchant_id][$location_id] = $jsonLine["location"];
        break;

      // received the availability chunk
      case "result":
        // get the result and just merge with location stored
        $arr_json[$merchant_id][$location_id] += $jsonLine["result"];
        break;
    }
  }
  if (!feof($file_handle)) {
    echo "Error: unexpected fgets() fail\n";
  }

  // close our stream handler
  fclose($file_handle);

  // send the new JSON block down to the client
```

```
    echo json_encode($arr_json);

}
?>
```

This is but one method for dealing with the chunked data return. Other options include using JSONP, which is supported by the Milo API. However, by including a helper web server you can also filter the results as needed and track the usage by your visitors.

As a business that is trying to get exposure to online customers, integrating and using the Milo API provides another avenue of reaching potential customers searching online: the customer can see that a storefront right around the corner has the product in stock, and see the current price. This can be compelling if the customer doesn't want to wait for (or pay for) the product to be shipped.

 A business can easily integrate and expose locations and inventories on Milo and third-party applications that use the Milo Open API by using a service called Milo Fetch. At the time of writing, the service is in beta form. It integrates with several third-party business administration and point-of-sale software packages, including Intuit QuickBooks Point of Sale, Pro, Premier, and Enterprise editions. See *http://pointof sale.milo.com* for more information.

See Also

Milo Open API Documentation (*https://www.x.com/developers/documentation-tools/milo/miloindex*)

Milo Open API Endpoints (*https://www.x.com/developers/documentation-tools/milo/endpoints.html*)

Milo Fetch (beta) (*https://pointofsale.milo.com/*)

1.3. Presenting Products Through eBay

Opportunity

When potential customers are searching online for a product, the main challenge a merchant faces is having its product offerings exposed and presented to those customers. Most of the time merchants rely on indexing of their sites and keywords to hopefully be mapped to online searches performed by people browsing the Internet. The more places that merchants can get their products indexed and listed, the greater potential there is for discovery by potential customers.

Solution

With a little effort, merchants can manually post products for auction and purchase on eBay by signing up for a seller account. This provides an opportunity for eBay users to discover the products. However, this is a manual process that is not integrated into the merchant's backend system. This example will show how an item can be added to eBay's marketplace by using the eBay Trading API and some simple calls. This model could then be employed to either automate or streamline the process.

Discussion

The eBay Trading API (*http://bit.ly/VO99WY*) is designed to work both in a sandbox and a production environment to search for items, retrieve category information, and add items. In this case we will use the `AddItem` call to programmatically add an item, with fields passed in an XML request that mimics adding an item manually. There are several fields in the `AddItem` request that are required, and additional fields that can be included based on the type of listing. eBay provides a full documentation set on the `AddItem` call, available in the eBay Trading API Call Reference (*http://bit.ly/12yutWn*).

This example will present the user with a brief form in which to enter the title of the item, the eBay category ID, the starting price, a URL of the item's picture, and a description, as seen in Figure 1-10. These are the core fields of an item listing.

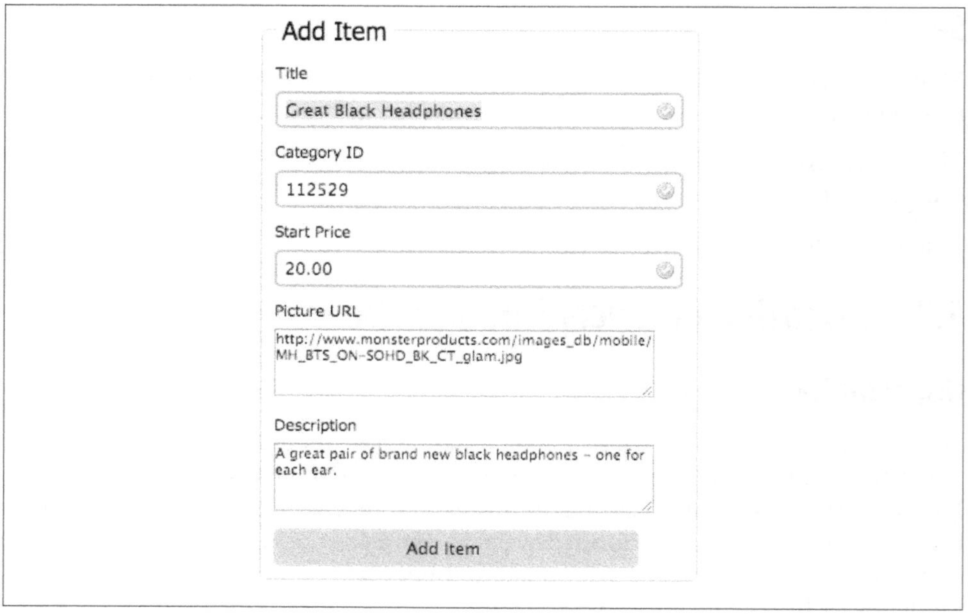

Figure 1-10. Add eBay item form

The *additem.php* page, which presents this form, will take the submitted fields and place them in an XML block to pass over in the AddItem call. In addition to these fields, there are a number of other fields that get included in the XML request. In this case, these fields have been left in the XML block and not brought into the form. When adapting this example to your needs, however, you may wish to change some of these fields, include others, or even allow the user to select the AddItem call fields in the form.

The eBay call reference page for the AddItem call describes each of the fields in detail and their possible values. For example, in the XML block of the *addItem.php* page you will find ConditionID, which is a numerical value representing the condition of the item (1000 is equal to "New" while 5000 is "Good"). For more information on working with the ConditionID field, you can reference the eBay document "Specifying an Item's Condition" (*http://bit.ly/R3MyIZ*). You could let the user select from a drop-down or choose a different value automatically. In this example, the item will be listed in an auction format, or in eBay terms as a "Chinese" auction, which is the standard auction type for eBay. You could change this to any of the other listing types that eBay provides; the full list of eBay listing types can be viewed in the eBay Trading API Call Reference (*http://bit.ly/UAkWsI*) online. Example 1-10 shows the *addItem.php* code.

Example 1-10. addItem.php

```php
<?php
/*******************************************
addItem.php

Uses eBay Trading API to list an item under
a seller's account.

*******************************************/

// include our Trading API constants
require_once 'tradingConstants.php';

// check if posted
if (!empty($_POST)) {

  // grab our posted keywords and call helper function
  // TODO: check if need urlencode
  $title = $_POST['title'];
  $categoryID = $_POST['categoryID'];
  $startPrice = $_POST['startPrice'];
  $pictureURL = $_POST['pictureURL'];
  $description = $_POST['description'];

  // call the getAddItem function to make AddItem call
  $response = getAddItem($title, $categoryID, $startPrice, $pictureURL,
    $description);

}
```

```
// function to call the Trading API AddItem
function getAddItem($addTitle, $addCatID, $addSPrice, $addPicture,
  $addDesc) {

  // create unique ID for adding item to prevent duplicate adds
  $uuid = md5(uniqid());

  // create the XML request
  $xmlRequest  = "<?xml version=\"1.0\" encoding=\"utf-8\"?>";
  $xmlRequest .= "<AddItemRequest
    xmlns=\"urn:ebay:apis:eBLBaseComponents\">";
  $xmlRequest .= "<ErrorLanguage>en_US</ErrorLanguage>";
  $xmlRequest .= "<WarningLevel>High</WarningLevel>";
  $xmlRequest .= "<Item>";
  $xmlRequest .= "<Title>" . $addTitle . "</Title>";
  $xmlRequest .= "<Description>" . $addDesc . "</Description>";
  $xmlRequest .= "<PrimaryCategory>";
  $xmlRequest .= "<CategoryID>" . $addCatID . "</CategoryID>";
  $xmlRequest .= "</PrimaryCategory>";
  $xmlRequest .= "<StartPrice>" . $addSPrice . "</StartPrice>";
  $xmlRequest .= "<ConditionID>1000</ConditionID>";
  $xmlRequest .= "<CategoryMappingAllowed>true
    </CategoryMappingAllowed>";
  $xmlRequest .= "<Country>US</Country>";
  $xmlRequest .= "<Currency>USD</Currency>";
  $xmlRequest .= "<DispatchTimeMax>3</DispatchTimeMax>";
  $xmlRequest .= "<ListingDuration>Days_7</ListingDuration>";
  $xmlRequest .= "<ListingType>Chinese</ListingType>";
  $xmlRequest .= "<PaymentMethods>PayPal</PaymentMethods>";
  $xmlRequest .= "<PayPalEmailAddress>yourpaypal@emailaddress.com
    </PayPalEmailAddress>";
  $xmlRequest .= "<PictureDetails>";
  $xmlRequest .= "<PictureURL>" . $addPicture . "</PictureURL>";
  $xmlRequest .= "</PictureDetails>";
  $xmlRequest .= "<PostalCode>05485</PostalCode>";
  $xmlRequest .= "<Quantity>1</Quantity>";
  $xmlRequest .= "<ReturnPolicy>";
  $xmlRequest .= "<ReturnsAcceptedOption>ReturnsAccepted
    </ReturnsAcceptedOption>";
  $xmlRequest .= "<RefundOption>MoneyBack</RefundOption>";
  $xmlRequest .= "<ReturnsWithinOption>Days_30</ReturnsWithinOption>";
  $xmlRequest .= "<Description>" . $addDesc . "</Description>";
  $xmlRequest .= "<ShippingCostPaidByOption>Buyer
    </ShippingCostPaidByOption>";
  $xmlRequest .= "</ReturnPolicy>";
  $xmlRequest .= "<ShippingDetails>";
  $xmlRequest .= "<ShippingType>Flat</ShippingType>";
  $xmlRequest .= "<ShippingServiceOptions>";
  $xmlRequest .= "<ShippingServicePriority>1
    </ShippingServicePriority>";
  $xmlRequest .= "<ShippingService>USPSMedia</ShippingService>";
```

```php
    $xmlRequest .= "<ShippingServiceCost>2.50</ShippingServiceCost>";
    $xmlRequest .= "</ShippingServiceOptions>";
    $xmlRequest .= "</ShippingDetails>";
    $xmlRequest .= "<Site>US</Site>";
    $xmlRequest .= "<UUID>" . $uuid . "</UUID>";
    $xmlRequest .= "</Item>";
    $xmlRequest .= "<RequesterCredentials>";
    $xmlRequest .= "<eBayAuthToken>" . AUTH_TOKEN . "</eBayAuthToken>";
    $xmlRequest .= "</RequesterCredentials>";
    $xmlRequest .= "<WarningLevel>High</WarningLevel>";
    $xmlRequest .= "</AddItemRequest>";

    // Define our header array for the Trading API call
    // Notice different headers from shopping API and SITE_ID
    // changes to SITEID
    $headers = array(
      'X-EBAY-API-SITEID:'.SITEID,
      'X-EBAY-API-CALL-NAME:AddItem',
      'X-EBAY-API-REQUEST-ENCODING:'.RESPONSE_ENCODING,
      'X-EBAY-API-COMPATIBILITY-LEVEL:' . API_COMPATIBILITY_LEVEL,
      'X-EBAY-API-DEV-NAME:' . API_DEV_NAME,
      'X-EBAY-API-APP-NAME:' . API_APP_NAME,
      'X-EBAY-API-CERT-NAME:' . API_CERT_NAME,
      'Content-Type: text/xml;charset=utf-8'
    );

    // initialize our curl session
    $session  = curl_init(API_URL);

    // set our curl options with the XML request
    curl_setopt($session, CURLOPT_HTTPHEADER, $headers);
    curl_setopt($session, CURLOPT_POST, true);
    curl_setopt($session, CURLOPT_POSTFIELDS, $xmlRequest);
    curl_setopt($session, CURLOPT_RETURNTRANSFER, true);

    // execute the curl request
    $responseXML = curl_exec($session);

    // close the curl session
    curl_close($session);

    // return the response XML
    return $responseXML;
}
?>

<!DOCTYPE html>
<html>
<head>
<meta charset="UTF-8" />
<title>1-4 Add Item to eBay using eBay Trading API</title>
<style>
body {background: #fff; color: #000;
```

```
      font: normal 62.5%/1.5 tahoma, verdana, sans-serif;}
* {margin: 0; padding: 0;}
form {padding: 0 10px; width: 700px;}
legend {font-size: 2em; padding-left: 5px; padding-right: 5px;
  position: relative;}
fieldset {border: 1px solid #ccc; border-radius: 5px; padding: 10px;
  width: 320px;}
li {clear: both; list-style-type: none; margin: 0 0 10px;}
label, input {font-size: 1.3em;}
label {display: block; padding: 0 0 5px; width: 200px;}
input {background-position: 295px 5px; background-repeat: no-repeat;
  border: 2px solid #ccc; border-radius: 5px;
  padding: 5px 25px 5px 5px; width: 285px;}
input:focus {outline: none;}
input:invalid:required {background-image: url(asterisk.png);
  box-shadow: none;}
input:focus:invalid {background-image: url(invalid.png);
  box-shadow: 0px 0px 5px #b01212; border: 2px solid #b01212;}
input:valid:required {background-image: url(accept.png);
  border: 2px solid #7ab526;}
div label {width: 100%;}
</style>
</head>
<body>
<div id="frmProduct">
  <!-- simple form for query keyword entry -->
  <form name="addItem" action="addItem.php" method="post">
    <fieldset>
    <legend>Add Item</legend>
    <ol>
      <li>
        <label for="title">Title</label>
        <input autofocus required id="title" name="title"
          value="Great Black Headphones" maxlength="80" />
      </li>
      <li>
        <label for="categoryID">Category ID</label>
        <input required id="categoryID" name="categoryID"
        value="112529"/>
      </li>
      <li>
        <label for="startPrice">Start Price</label>
        <input required id="startPrice" name="startPrice"
          value="20.00"/>
      </li>
      <li>
        <label for="pictureURL">Picture URL</label>
        <textarea rows="4" cols="40" required id="pictureURL"
          name="pictureURL">http://www.monsterproducts.com/images_db/
          mobile/MH_BTS_ON-SOHD_BK_CT_glam.jpg</textarea>
      </li>
      <li>
```

```
          <label for="description">Description</label>
          <textarea rows="4" cols="40" required id="description"
            name="description">A great pair of brand new black
            headphones - one for each ear.</textarea>
        </li>
      </ol>
      <input type="submit" value="Add Item">
      </fieldset>
      <br/>
    </form>
  </div>
</div>
<div id="container">

  <?php
    // display information to user based on AddItem response

    // convert the XML response string in an XML object
    $xmlResponse = simplexml_load_string($response);

    // verify that the XML response object was created
    if ($xmlResponse) {

      // check for call success
      if ($xmlResponse->Ack == "Success") {

        // display the item ID number added
        echo "<p>Successfully added item as item #" .
          $xmlResponse->ItemID . "<br/>";

        // calculate fees for listing
        // loop through each Fee block in the Fees child node
        $totalFees = 0;
        $fees = $xmlResponse->Fees;
        foreach ($fees->Fee as $fee) {
          $totalFees += $fee->Fee;
        }
        echo "Total Fees for this listing: " . $totalFees . ".</p>";

      } else {

        // unsuccessful call, display error(s)
        echo "<p>The AddItem called failed due to the following
          error(s):<br/>";
        foreach ($xmlResponse->Errors as $error) {
          $errCode = $error->ErrorCode;
          $errLongMsg = htmlentities($error->LongMessage);
          $errSeverity = $error->SeverityCode;
          echo $errSeverity . ": [" . $errCode . "] " .
            $errLongMsg . "<br/>";
        }
        echo "</p>";
```

```
        }

    }
?>
</div>
</body>
</html>
```

To get the appropriate eBay category ID that is required for adding an item, you can use the `GetCategories` Trading API call (*http://developer.ebay.com/devzone/xml/docs/refer ence/ebay/GetCategories.html*) [and test it with the API Test Tool, as described in Recipe 1.1, "Tapping Into Product Reviews and Guides"]. In this example, the appropriate category ID has been included directly in the XML request. This is fine if you are listing only one type of item that always fits into a single category, but you will most likely want to incorporate the `GetCategories` call into your own solution.

In addition to the fields already mentioned as required, there are two other fields worth describing in the `AddItem` call. The first is a universally unique ID, or UUID. For the `AddItem` call, this UUID field takes a 32-hex-character string. This value must be different for each `AddItem` call that is made. The purpose of this field is to prevent duplication of calls, which could add the same item more than once. In the example here, a simple MD5 hash of the output of the `uniqid` PHP function is used to produce this ID.

The last field that will be specific to your call is the `eBayAuthToken`, and it is critical to the request. The auth token represents the authorization of the eBay user on whose behalf this call is made in your application to access eBay data. To get an auth token for a single user—for example, if you will be adding items for only a single merchant in-house or you are testing in the sandbox—you can use the User Token Tool (*https:// developer.ebay.com/DevZone/account/tokens/default.aspx*) in the eBay Developer Tools. With this tool, you can generate an auth token for a single user in the sandbox or production environment and create a sandbox user to test with, as seen in Figure 1-11.

 When creating a sandbox user, use a real email address to which you have access. eBay listing confirmation messages from the sandbox environment will be sent to this email address.

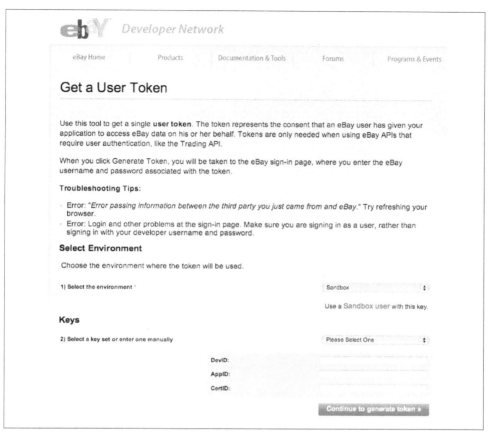

Figure 1-11. Creating an eBay user token

If you are creating an item-listing tool, you will need to get the auth token programmatically for the eBay user using your application. For more information on programmatically acquiring a user's authorization and fetching the token for your application, see the online eBay Trading API tutorial, "Getting Tokens" (*http://bit.ly/ZKRPcf*).

After getting your auth token, place the token string and app credentials in the *trading Constants.php* file. These constants are used in the HTTP headers and the XML request for the *addItem.php* page. Example 1-11 shows the *tradingConstants.php* file with sample sandbox credentials set.

Example 1-11. tradingConstants.php

```php
<?php
/*********************************************
tradingConstants.php

Constants used for Trading API calls.
Replace keys and tokens with your information.

*********************************************/

// eBay site to use - 0 = United States
DEFINE("SITEID",0);

// production vs. sandbox flag - true=production
DEFINE("FLAG_PRODUCTION",false);

// eBay Trading API version to use
DEFINE("API_COMPATIBILITY_LEVEL",779);

/* Set the Dev, App, and Cert IDs.
Create these on developer.ebay.com.
Check if need to use production or sandbox keys. */
if (FLAG_PRODUCTION) {

  // PRODUCTION
  // set the production URL for Trading API calls
  DEFINE("API_URL",'https://api.ebay.com/ws/api.dll');

  // set production credentials (from developer.ebay.com)
  DEFINE("API_DEV_NAME",'<YOUR_PRODUCTION_DEV_ID>');
  DEFINE("API_APP_NAME",'<YOUR_PRODUCTION_APP_ID>');
  DEFINE("API_CERT_NAME",'<YOUR_PRODUCTION_CERT_ID>');

  // set the auth token for the user profile used
  DEFINE("AUTH_TOKEN",'<YOUR_PRODUCTION_TOKEN>');

} else {

  // SANDBOX
  // set the sandbox URL for Trading API calls
  DEFINE("API_URL",'https://api.sandbox.ebay.com/ws/api.dll');

  // set sandbox credentials (from developer.ebay.com)
  DEFINE("API_DEV_NAME",'48242bdb-6e6e-4a84-bba9-aaaaaaaaaaaa');
  DEFINE("API_APP_NAME",bbbbbbbbb-ff13-407f-993c-3fd6de0e3c27');
  DEFINE("API_CERT_NAME",'45daa688-54ec-cccc-cccc-b72247092fba');

  // set the auth token for the user profile used
  DEFINE("AUTH_TOKEN",'AgAAAA**AQAAAA**aAAAAA**8L/9Tw**nY+sHZ2PrBmd
    j6wVnY+sEZ2PrA2dj6wFk4GhCZCLow6dj6x9nY+seQ**7bgAAA**AAMAAA**MrJ
    m8FW/aMCMHEJUpxoPu3lbx3moJHLrO6E3dIJmN6Y7ljWtD0EMM/TKSS26K1IaSp
```

Z4JR4pZ5YelGOS5z571BsPwokbcdcy/G4wDHxF3DWXfh8uEUY3j/R4VOY2h4VzU
9sNLl6iXdMRvtm9Td7M4artDSiecqiR1JUv+Oy3OSI5XevHGY0RSEDt+...');
```
}
?>
```

After the form on the *addItem.php* page is submitted with the basic listing information, the `AddItem` Trading API call is made using the merged fields in the request XML block. The `AddItem` call will return an XML block similar to the one shown in Example 1-12 if successful. The return XML will contain an `Ack` element to flag whether the call was a `Success` or had a `Failure`. If a failure occurred, the return XML will contain the error causing the failure. In a successful call, summary information will be contained in the response, including the resulting eBay item ID and start and end times for the listing. In addition, the return block will include a section of fees representing the individual costs for the added item.

Example 1-12. Sample AddItem return XML

```xml
<?xml version="1.0" encoding="UTF-8"?>
<AddItemResponse xmlns="urn:ebay:apis:eBLBaseComponents">
  <Timestamp>2012-07-12T00:01:43.177Z</Timestamp>
  <Ack>Success</Ack>
  <Version>779</Version>
  <Build>E779_CORE_BUNDLED_15043314_R1</Build>
  <ItemID>110100620547</ItemID>
  <StartTime>2012-07-12T00:01:42.817Z</StartTime>
  <EndTime>2012-07-19T00:01:42.817Z</EndTime>
  <Fees>
    <Fee>
      <Name>AuctionLengthFee</Name>
      <Fee currencyID="USD">0.0</Fee>
    </Fee>
    <Fee>
      <Name>BoldFee</Name>
      ...
      ...
    <Fee>
      <Name>MotorsGermanySearchFee</Name>
      <Fee currencyID="USD">0.0</Fee>
    </Fee>
  </Fees>
  <DiscountReason>SpecialOffer</DiscountReason>
</AddItemResponse>
```

The *addItem.php* page will check the return XML for success via the `Ack` field, and if it's found to be successful, will display the item ID and the total fees paid to list the item. If this functionality were being included in an automated listing application, the item ID, fees, and start and end times returned could be stored for further automation and viewing.

Figure 1-12 shows the resulting listing for our sample item.

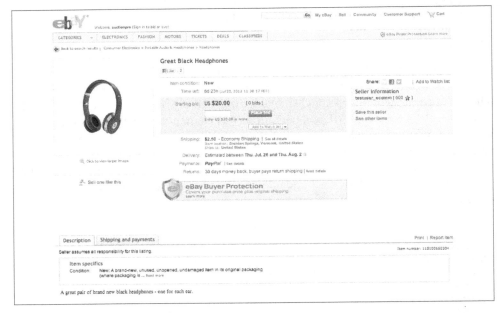

Figure 1-12. Resulting eBay listing

To manually validate that the item was listed, you can search for the item ID returned on the *addItem.php* page on the eBay site. The `GetItem` Trading API call can also be used to present the same item details to the user.

With some simple programming, you can make a custom entry form for your staff to add products more easily, integrate your inventory into the eBay site, and even do batches of listings, potentially creating more traffic for your site and boosting sales of your products.

See Also

eBay Trading API (*https://www.x.com/developers/ebay/products/trading-api*)

eBay Trading API AddItem call reference (*http://developer.ebay.com/DevZone/XML/docs/Reference/eBay/AddItem.html*)

eBay Trading API GetCategories call reference (*http://developer.ebay.com/devzone/xml/docs/reference/ebay/GetCategories.html*)

API Test Tool (*https://developer.ebay.com/DevZone/build-test/test-tool/default.aspx*)

1.4. Conclusion

The first step of the commerce lifecycle—product discovery and research—can be one of the most difficult to get past since customers have so many options for finding goods on the Internet. The examples contained in this chapter show the possibilities of providing product reviews inline, displaying local purchase options if available, and adding products to eBay programmatically. By incorporating features such as these into your own commerce practices, you can increase the number of users who start the commerce lifecycle and the number of people who move on to the second step of the simplified commerce lifecycle described here.

CHAPTER 2

Product Presentation

In the last chapter we considered step one of the simplified commerce lifecycle, where a potential customer discovers your product or service. The challenge for a vendor is to provide the information necessary to allow for a quick and simple purchase decision by the visitor. How the product is presented to the user can greatly influence the likelihood of getting to the next step in the simplified commerce lifecycle illustrated in Figure 2-1: purchasing.

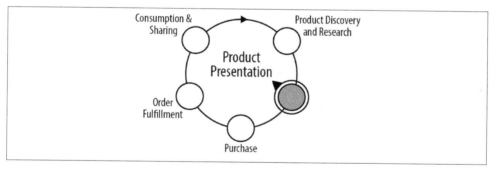

Figure 2-1. Simplified commerce lifecycle—stage 2

In this chapter the examples will show how, with proper presentation techniques and incorporating concepts such as social commerce, single sign-on, and cross selling, a vendor can increase the chance of a customer making the decision to purchase. In the first recipe we will incorporate the Facebook Open Graph API with the X.commerce services to incorporate social commerce into a Magento storefront. User feedback of "want" and "use" of products from the Open Graph will be incorporated into the product page.

The next recipe will show how, with minimal effort, you can incorporate the PayPal Access and Identity offerings to provide a single sign-on for a user with that user's PayPal credentials and retrieve basic user profile information. In this manner you can customize your product presentation without having to ask the user to set multiple configuration options.

Lastly, we will look at the potential of cross-selling or up-selling a customer with similar items presented from eBay with the eBay Merchandising API. Overall, these examples can increase conversion rates and the number of customers moving on in the simplified commerce lifecycle.

2.1. Customizing a Magento Storefront

Opportunity

The Magento commerce platform is a powerful engine with many features for creating an online storefront quickly and easily. However, presenting products and incorporating social feedback can still be a challenge. Social commerce, or the use of social feeds, websites, and recommendations by social contacts, can have a profound impact on increasing user engagement and click-through sales. The incorporation of the Facebook Open Graph into a Magento storefront can fuel this social commerce opportunity.

Solution

One of the robust architecture features of Magento is the capability of the platform to add functionality through extensions developed by you or one of the developers in the Magento community. Developers can create extensions to enhance the present functionality of the storefront or to incorporate outside features or websites into the application. In this example, a free extension (Facebook Open Graph 2.0) will be used to incorporate actions such as "I use" and "I want" between the Facebook Open Graph and Magento. The end result is that users will see Facebook buttons on product pages to mark products they use or want, and these attributions will appear on the product pages and the users' Facebook accounts.

Discussion

"Social commerce" is a term that has been used to describe the intersection of the social spectrum with vendors and their products or services. By incorporating the social graph, where members of the community can express positive feedback for items they like or want, vendors can increase sales through word of mouth and brand recognition. The Facebook Open Graph API provides integration into the social feeds of Facebook, and when it is combined with the messaging potential of the X.commerce services and the product catalog of Magento, a powerful social commerce engine can be created.

The Magento ecommerce platform provides for this type of integration and collaborative data sharing through the use of extensions. Published extensions from developers can be found in the Magento Extension Marketplace or Magento Connect (*http:// www.magentocommerce.com/magento-connect*). For this example, the implementation will leverage a free extension from Magento that incorporates the Facebook Open Graph functionality and the X.commerce Fabric messaging and data retrieval features. The extension is named Facebook Open Graph 2.0 (*http://www.magentocommerce.com/ magento-connect/facebook-open-graph-2-0.html*), and when installed it will be listed under the Social Commerce section in the Magento configuration.

> If as a developer you are interested in creating your own extension to the Magento system, documentation including the downloadable Magento Connect Extension Developer's Guidelines (*http://www.magento commerce.com/magento-connect/create_your_extension/*) is available online at the Magento Commerce site, with detailed steps for developing and packaging your extension.

Before you get started with installing the Facebook extension into your Magento implementation, make sure that your Magento version is one of the compatible versions for the extension. Compatible versions are listed on the extension page in the Magento Extension Marketplace (*http://bit.ly/12yv8qK*).

To integrate the Facebook Open Graph 2.0 extension, this example is broken down into the following seven steps:

1. Install the *xcom* prerequisite extension in Magento.
2. Install the Facebook Open Graph 2.0 extension.
3. Configure a new app in your Facebook account.
4. Create an X.commerce account and authorization file.
5. Authorize the extension with X.commerce.
6. Create the Open Graph Facebook object and actions.
7. Create the same actions in the extension, and launch.

The Facebook extension requires the installation of the xcom PHP extension into your system. The xcom extension handles communication with the X.commerce services and provides the core methods by which the Facebook extension communicates with Magento. The xcom extension is available through PECL or GitHub (*https://github.com/ johnj/php5-xcom*). To install the xcom extension on your system, clone the project from GitHub by performing the following command on your Magento server:

```
git clone git://github.com/johnj/php5-xcom.git
```

After cloning the Git repository, perform the following commands:

```
phpize
./configure
make install
```

The xcom extension should now be installed on your system as a prerequisite for running the Facebook extension.

 In order to compile and install the xcom extension, your system will need *libavro*. *libavro* is a remote procedure call and serialization framework that is used in the xcom extension for messaging. If your system does not have *libavro* installed, you will need to follow the steps below to retrieve the library from the Git *avro* repository, make the package, and install it. The *avro* library uses CMake to build:

```
git clone https://github.com/johnj/avro.git
cd avro/lang/c
cmake .
sudo make install
```

To perform step 2 and install the Facebook extension into your Magento implementation, you will first need to get an extension key from Magento Connect for the Facebook extension. On the Facebook Open Graph 2.0 (*http://www.magentocommerce.com/magento-connect/facebook-open-graph-2-0.html*) extension page in Magento Connect, select your platform and click "Install Now." Then select your Magento Connect version, agree to the extension license agreement, and click "Get Extension Key." An extension key similar to the following will be displayed: *http://connect20.magentocommerce.com/community/Social_Facebook*. The specific key that you receive may be different based on your platform and Connect version. Copy the extension key and store it for later, as you will use it in your Magento administration console to install and activate the Facebook extension.

Next, log into the Magento administration console of your implementation and go to System → Magento Connect → Magento Connect Manager. In the "Install New Extensions" section, paste the extension key retrieved from Magento Connect for the Facebook extension and click "Install," as shown in Figure 2-2.

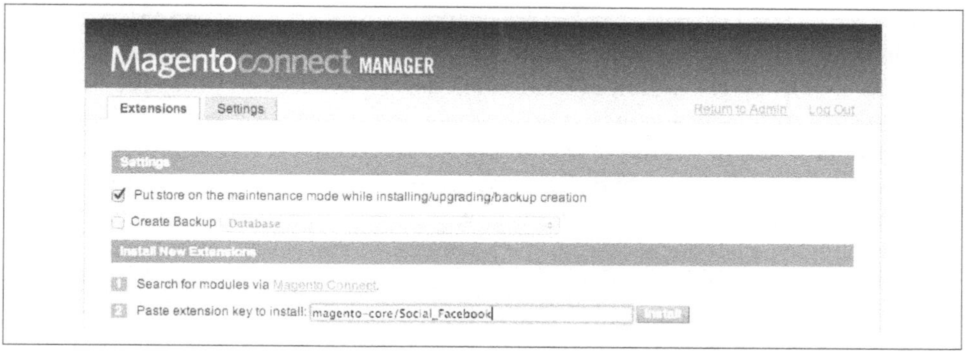

Figure 2-2. Installing new extensions in Magento Connect

After installation, the extension should be listed in the existing extensions list on the same page under the title *Social_Facebook*. Click "Return to Admin" and go to the System → Configuration menu, where you should now see a new configuration area titled "SOCIAL COMMERCE → X.commerce & Facebook," as seen in Figure 2-3. If you do not see the new configuration submenu, log out of Magento and log back into the administration console. The menu option should now be shown.

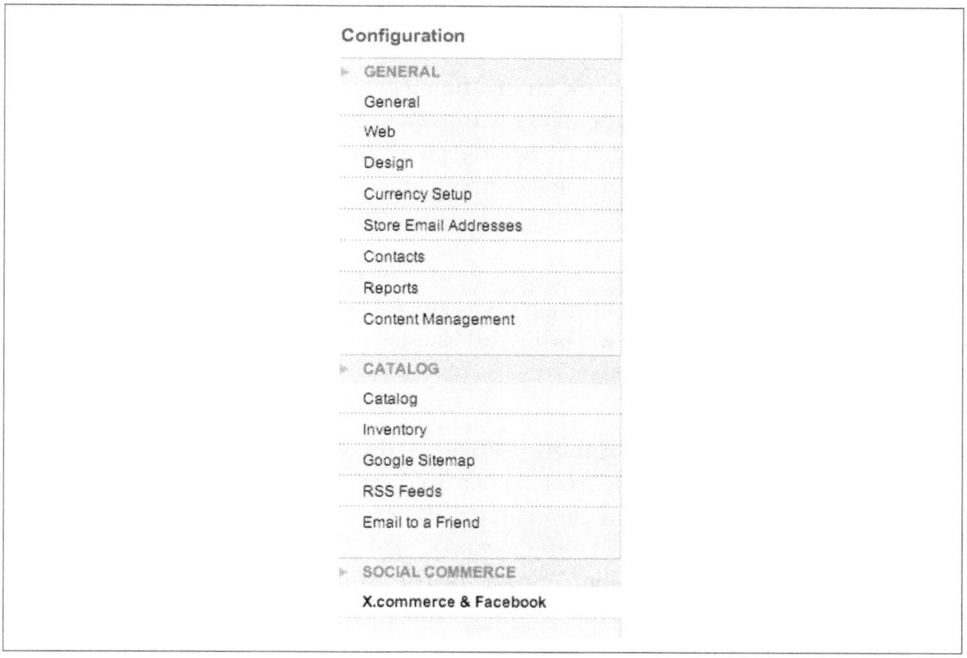

Figure 2-3. Extension installed in System → Configuration

For step 3, you need to create the Facebook app that will integrate into this extension and allow the extension to communicate with the Facebook Open Graph API. To add a new Facebook app you will need a Facebook developer account, which is authorized to create apps. You may be required by Facebook to further validate your account, but the developer access will be free of charge. Once your account is authorized, go to *http:// developers.facebook.com/apps* and click "Create New App." A dialog will be shown where you can enter your app name and namespace, as shown in Figure 2-4. The web hosting selection should be left unchecked, as the X.commerce messaging service will be leveraged for the application. After selecting a name and namespace for the app, click "Continue."

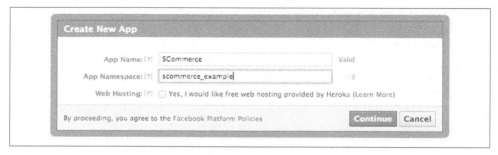

Figure 2-4. Creating a new app in Facebook

After the initial dialog on Facebook for creating a new app, you will be asked to enter the basic information for the app along with the app domains (Figure 2-5). The app domains should contain the domain that corresponds to your Magento implementation. In the bottom portion of the form, make sure to add the same domain into the section "Website with Facebook Login."

 Take note of the app ID, app secret, and namespace for your Facebook app, as these fields will be needed later to configure the Facebook extension in Magento.

After filling out the rest of the form, click "Save Changes." An X.commerce account and authorization file will need to be created next. To do so, return to the Magento Administration console and go to the X.commerce & Facebook configuration settings, under System → Configuration. On the configuration screen of the extension, click "Generate an X.commerce Authorization File." You will then be taken to the X.commerce Extension Center, as shown in Figure 2-6.

SCommerce
App ID: 415997175120115
App Secret: da8cee7b98c6ce4d841776932e02c1a5 (reset)

Basic Info

Display Name: [?]	SCommerce
Namespace: [?]	scommerce_example
Contact Email: [?]	johnjawed@gmail.com
App Domains: [?]	Enter your site domains and press enter
Category: [?]	Other ▾ Choose a sub-category ▾
Hosting URL: [?]	You have not generated a URL through one of our partners (Get one)
Sandbox Mode: [?]	○ Enabled ⊙ Disabled

Select how your app integrates with Facebook

✓ Website with Facebook Login	Log in to my website using Facebook.
✓ App on Facebook	Use my app inside Facebook.com.
✓ Mobile Web	Bookmark my web app on Facebook mobile.
✓ Native iOS App	Publish from my iOS app to Facebook.
✓ Native Android App	Publish from my Android app to Facebook.
✓ Page Tab	Build a custom tab for Facebook Pages.

Save Changes

Figure 2-5. Completed Facebook app registration

 Note that sometimes the X.commerce, Facebook, and Magento interfaces may become confused with session management. If you do not get the expected screen in this flow, log out of the site you're in, close the window or tab in your browser, and try again. For example, if you do not get the X.commerce Extension Authorization Center page when trying to generate an authorization file, click the "Log Out" link, close the window or tab, and try again from the Magento interface.

Click the Login button to continue. After logging into the X.commerce area you will be asked to create an X.commerce Merchant Account, if you do not already have one. Fill in the appropriate information as shown in Figure 2-7 and continue.

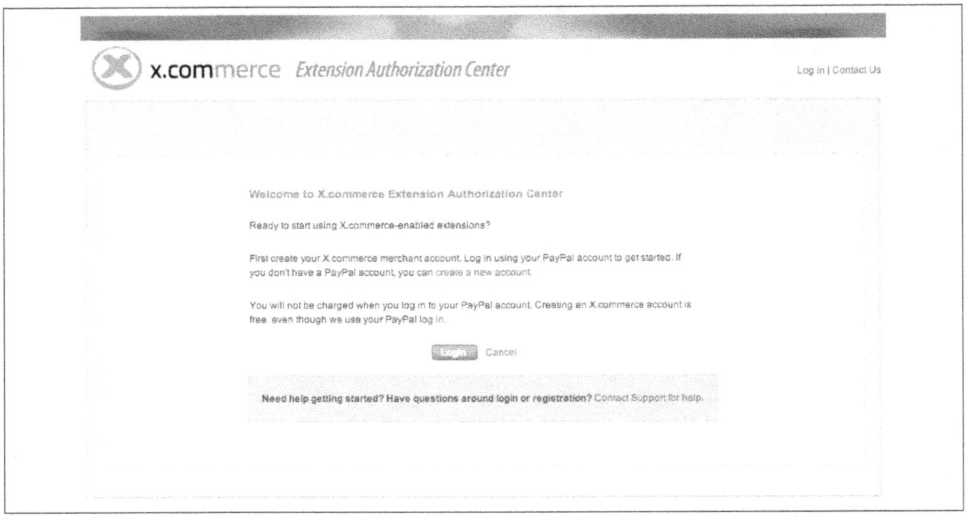

Figure 2-6. Extension Authorization Center login

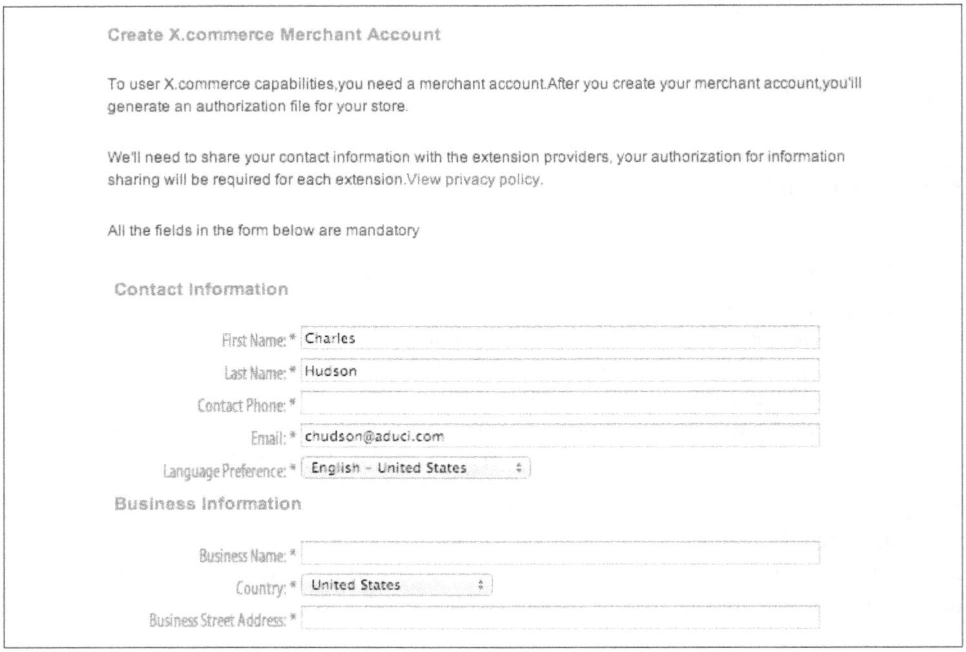

Figure 2-7. X.commerce Merchant Account creation form

Once the form is complete and you have confirmed the information, the authorization file can be generated. Enter your store name as shown in Figure 2-8. The store name can be any name corresponding to your storefront that you wish.

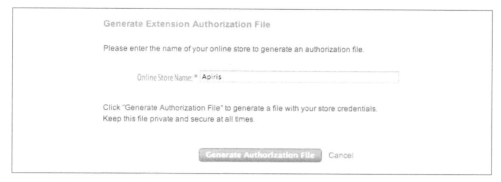

Figure 2-8. Generating the authorization file

Click "Generate Authorization File" and a download of your authorization file will begin. The file downloaded will have an *.auth* extension and will be named after your store, similar to *Apiris_50786b489353d.auth*.

Once the file has been downloaded, return to the Social Commerce extension settings and upload the authentication file. After successfully uploading the file, a "Current Token" field should be displayed, as seen in Figure 2-9.

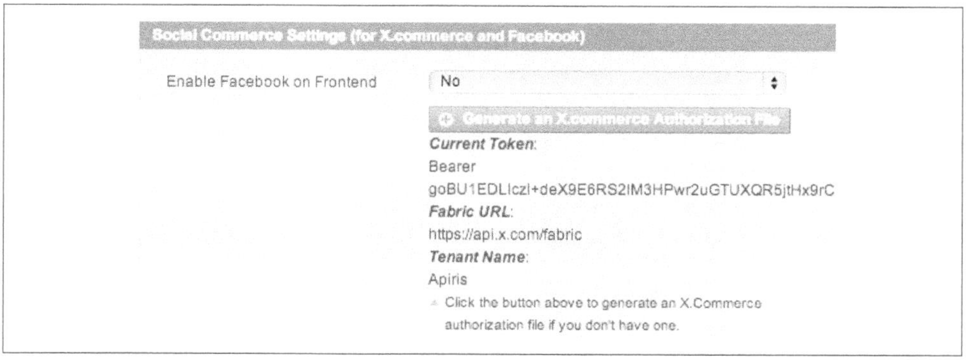

Figure 2-9. Successful authorization file upload

Once you've uploaded the authorization file you will need to authorize the Social Commerce extension with X.com, or X.commerce Fabric. Click the "Authorize the Social Commerce Extension" button, as shown in Figure 2-10. This will open the X.commerce authorization window.

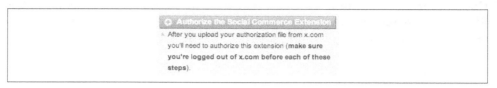

Figure 2-10. Authorizing the social commerce extension

If you are not brought to the expected "Authorize Social Commerce Extension" page, as seen in Figure 2-11, log out of X.commerce, close the window, and try again.

Figure 2-11. Authorizing the extension on X.commerce

Select the checkbox to authorize the extension, and then click the "Authorize Extension" button. This concludes step 5, to authorize the extension with the X.commerce services.

The last two steps are to map the available objects and actions that will be integrated with the Facebook Open Graph. First you will need to set up the object and actions for the Facebook app. Next, the same object and action will need to be tied into the Magento Social Commerce extension settings so the two match.

 An *Object* for the Open Graph can reference any type of object, but for most Magento implementations it will typically be a *Product* or *Service*. However, if your Magento product catalog consists only of video games, as an example, your object may instead be a *Game*. In this manner the proper messaging can be displayed, such as "I play this game" or "I want this game."

In the Facebook developers area, open the Open Graph settings for your Facebook app by clicking on "Open Graph" in the menu, as seen in Figure 2-12. Define the action and product for the app by entering what people can do with the product. Click "Get Started" to continue with the wizard to configure the action and object.

Figure 2-12. Open Graph settings

Define the action name, as seen in Figure 2-13, and continue through the wizard with the defaults.

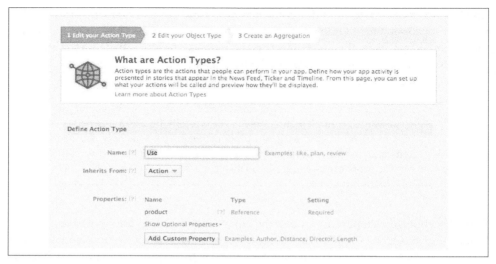

Figure 2-13. Defining the action type

After completing the action and object configuration wizard, the resulting object and action will be shown on the dashboard. Next, you need to add this same action into the Magento Social Commerce extension. In the administration settings for the extension at the bottom of the page, click "Add an Action" and enter the Facebook action and button title to display, as seen in Figure 2-14.

Figure 2-14. Extension action settings

Now that the relationships are set between the Magento extension, Facebook, and X.commerce, the extension can be enabled in Magento. At the top of the settings, select "Yes" from the "Enable Facebook on Frontend" drop-down, as seen in Figure 2-15, to enable the extension.

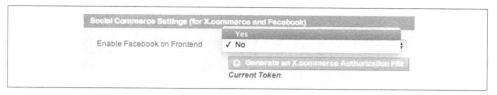

Figure 2-15. Enabling the extension

You have now reached the end of the seven steps, and hopefully you were able to follow along fairly easily. Now it's time to test the added social component and see how it looks on the product pages of your site. On your Magento storefront, navigate to a particular product page. You should see on your product page the social commerce extension embedded with the action or actions that you have defined, as in Figure 2-16.

Figure 2-16. Embedded social commerce extension view

If you get an error stating that the X.commerce extension was not loaded, as shown in Figure 2-17, the issue stems from not having the *libavro* library installed. This is a necessary component for running the xcom extension installed at the beginning of this example. You will need to install the *libavro* library to correct the error.

This example shows how, with some installed extensions but no coding, you can add a social element to your Magento storefront to bring in recommendations and create brand awareness among Facebook social circles.

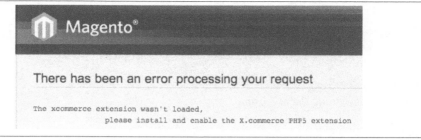

Figure 2-17. Error display without libavro dependency

See Also

Magento Connect – Facebook Open Graph 2.0 (*http://www.magentocommerce.com/magento-connect/facebook-open-graph-2-0.html*)

Social Commerce with Magento & Facebook (*http://prezi.com/pocorwswf_dj/social-commerce/*)

Facebook Developers Site (*https://developers.facebook.com/*)

X.commerce Fabric Developer Package (*https://www.x.com/developers/x.commerce/products/x.commerce-developer-package*)

X.commerce Messaging: Advanced Method Using Magento (*https://www.x.com/developers/x.commerce/how-to-guides/x.commerce-messaging-advanced-method-using-magento*)

2.2. Personalizing a Store Experience

Opportunity

Creating and securing user login information can be challenging, not only for merchants but also for the customers who have to remember credentials across several websites. With secure systems and protocols such as OpenID Connect, there is the opportunity to provide a form of single sign-on across multiple websites. Customers can then rely on a universal login, while merchants can leverage an outside party for user authentication. In turn, once the customer is logged in, merchants can provide more custom information with the products presented.

Solution

In an OpenID Connect model, a user chooses to log into a website using an ID that has been registered with a third party. The user is passed over to the third-party login interface to validate her account, and the credentials are securely returned to the referring site. Third-party OpenID Connect providers include Google, PayPal, and Yahoo!. By default, with PayPal's Access offering for OpenID Connect, users can log into your site through PayPal's Access control and be authenticated via the OpenID Connect support for PayPal Access. This allows the user to sign in quickly and securely and to share profile information with the site if she so chooses.

Discussion

This example will use the PayPal Access API to provide a login to users, allowing them to authenticate using their PayPal credentials. The user will be provided with a button to click to log in via PayPal. When clicked, the button will launch a secure login window from PayPal. If the user successfully logs in, PayPal will ask if he wishes to allow sharing of profile information with the referring website. If the user agrees, the login window is closed and the user is returned to the referring website and logged in—with the website knowing a little more about the user so the user experience can be customized. The benefits of this streamlined user experience include:

Customization
> Increased opportunities to customize the product presentation based on the knowledge of the user.

Peace of mind
> An increased comfort level for the user through PayPal brand recognition.

Security
> Increased security for the merchant, since PayPal handles the account login information.

Convenience
> A new account is not required; the user needs to remember only a single account.

From the user's point of view, using PayPal login credentials to securely sign into multiple websites is quick and simple. But behind the scenes the process is a bit more complex, with care taken to assure that the flow is seamless and, most importantly, secure through the use of OpenID Connect and OAuth 2 for the protocol.

> OpenID Connect is preferred over OpenID for implementing PayPal Access, due to its higher security standards.

In Figure 2-18 the flow for this example is shown, including the retrieval of secure tokens and user profile information that the code in this example will perform.

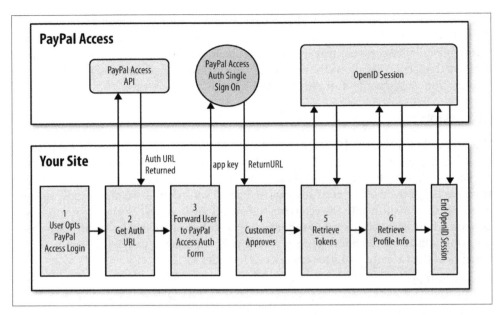

Figure 2-18. Access flow to log in and retrieve profile information

In the flow in Figure 2-18 you can see that multiple calls have to take place to the PayPal Access API to authenticate the user and retrieve the profile information. In this example the process involves the following steps:

1. The user is presented with a PayPal Access login button pulled from the PayPal servers.

2. A request is made to the PayPal Access API for the authentication URL to pass the user to.

3. A window is opened with the authentication URL.

4. After completing the sign-in on the authentication URL from PayPal, the user is returned to a return URL on your domain.

5. Now that the user has been authenticated and allowed your site access to his OpenID Connect profile, authentication and access tokens can be retrieved from an OpenID Connect session.

6. With the tokens returned, the user's OpenID Connect profile information can be retrieved.

7. After retrieving the user's profile, the OpenID Connect session is closed.

For a merchant, the benefits of using the PayPal Access and OpenID Connect model of user authentication not only include validating the user against a known entity such as

PayPal, but also that the merchant can request profile information about the user from PayPal. The code in this example will retrieve the OpenID Connect demographic profile information of the user, as well as the user's email address and physical address. The OpenID Connect components that are retrieved are considered the *scope* of the data to be shared with the website and must be set up and requested by the website.

On the development side, the first step is to sign into the X.commerce Developer Portal (*http://bit.ly/ZgK3ru*) and register an application for use with the PayPal Access services. In Figure 2-19, the form for registering your new application is shown.

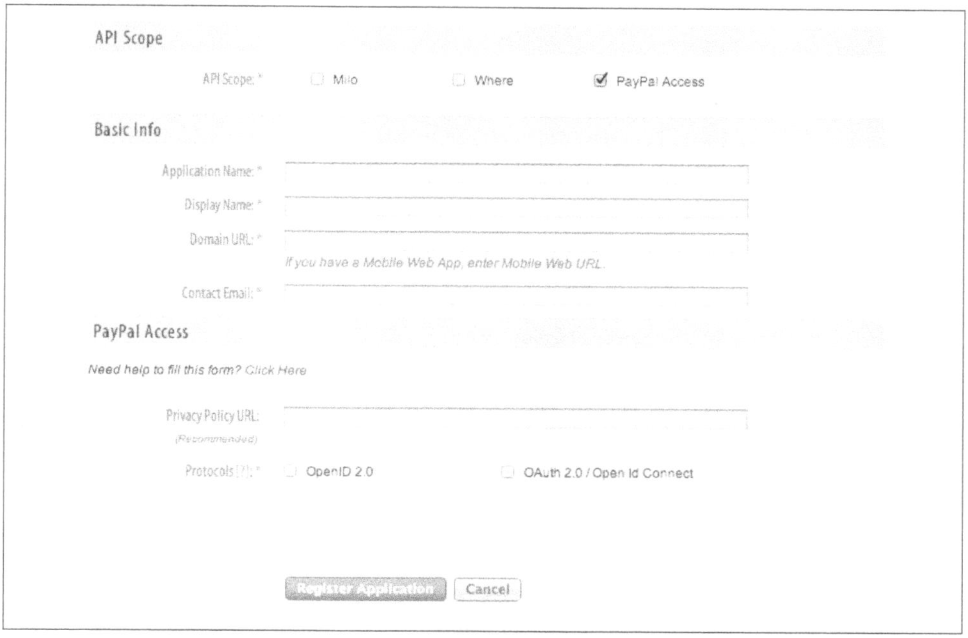

Figure 2-19. X.com application registration form

In the form for registering your application, select "PayPal Access" for the API Scope to be used. Then provide an application name and a display name. The display name is what will be shown to the user on the PayPal login pages. In the Protocols section under "PayPal Access," make sure to select "OAuth 2.0 / Open Id Connect." When you select this combination, you will be asked for the return URL and attributes level for access. The return URL is the page to which the user is returned upon completion of the PayPal sign-on form. This will be the page on your site that will handle opening the OpenID Connect session and retrieving the tokens and profile information. In this example the page is named *authReturn.php*. The attributes level corresponds to the OpenID Connect attributes that you wish to have access to on your site. For this example you can select all the attributes, for testing purposes.

In a production version of this example the OpenID Connect attributes selected in the application registration form should be the minimum set that you need, to minimize security risks. In this example we have selected all the attributes for demonstration purposes only.

After completing the registration of your application, you will be provided with an *app ID* (also known as an *app key*) and *app secret*. You will need to pass this key and secret over to the PayPal Access service with your requests for authentication. Figure 2-20 shows the registered application with the app ID and secret.

Figure 2-20. Registered application details

Now that you've registered the application for use with the PayPal Access service, you can add to your site the code to talk with the service. To begin, download the initial code kit from GitHub (*https://github.com/paypal/paypal-access/tree/master/openid-connect-php-ppaccess*). Make sure to download the *openid-connect-php-ppaccess* folder to match the protocols and PHP language used in this example. The folder will contain two files, *auth.php* and *example.php*. This example will use only the *auth.php* file, which is the communication class for handling the PHP curl and JSON calls to the PayPal Access service.

Inside *auth.php*, the application key and secret are also kept for making the calls to the PayPal Access service. You will need to update these two items in the heading of the class, along with the scopes and return_url variables. Example 2-1 shows the header of the class with the fields that need to be replaced. For this example the return URL should match your domain and the *authReturn.php* filename.

Example 2-1. auth.php variables to be set

```
class PayPalAccess{
    private $key = '<YOUR_APP_KEY>';
    private $secret = '<YOUR_APP_SECRET>';
    private $scopes = 'openid profile email address';
    private $state;
    private $return_url = '<YOUR_URL>/authReturn.php';
```

The scopes variable contains the OpenID Connect scopes that are going to be requested to be shared from the OpenID Connect service to the website making the request. You should change the value to 'openid profile email address', which informs the OpenID Connect service that you would like the user's demographic profile information, email address, and physical address. The possible scopes include profile, email, address, and phone. The list must start with openid and contain a space-delimited list of the scopes being requested. The scopes are based on the OpenID Connect specification (*http://openid.net/specs/openid-connect-basic-1_0.html*). Once these class variables are set for the PayPalAccess object class, you can save the *auth.php* file.

Next, the page that will display the PayPal Access login button needs to be created. This page will also display the user's profile information after login. Example 2-2 contains the code for the *ppaccess_example.php* page.

Example 2-2. ppaccess_example.php example page

```
<?php
/*********************************************
ppaccess_example.php

Example launch file showing if the customer
has logged in via the PayPal Identity service.
If the user has not logged in, a login button
is provided that will launch the auth URL.
```

```php
   Once logged in, the token and profile info are
   shown.
   *********************************************/

   // Start our session.
   session_start();

   // Require the auth class.
   require_once('auth.php');

   // Handle actions selected.
   if (isset($_GET['action'])) {
     if ($_GET['action'] = 'logout') {
       // Clean up session and flags.
       unset($_SESSION['TOKEN']);
       unset($_SESSION['PROFILE']);
       $flgLoggedIn = false;
     }
   }

   // Check if the user is logged in.
   if (isset($_SESSION['TOKEN'])) {

     // User logged in, set flag.
     $flgLoggedIn = true;

   } else {

     // User not logged in, set flag.
     $flgLoggedIn = false;
     // Initialize a new PayPal Access instance.
     $ppaccess = new PayPalAccess();
     // Get the authentication URL for logging in.
     $auth_url = $ppaccess->get_auth_url();
   }

   ?>
   <!DOCTYPE html>
   <html>
   <head>
   <title>PayPal Access OpenID Connect</title>
   <style>
   * {margin: 0; padding: 0;}
   body {background: #fff; color: #000;
     font: normal 62.5%/1.5 tahoma, verdana, sans-serif;}
   legend {font-size: 2em; padding-left: 5px; padding-right: 5px;
     position: relative;}
   fieldset {border: 1px solid #ccc; border-radius: 5px; float: left;
     padding: 10px; margin: 10px; width: 320px;}
   li {clear: both; list-style-type: none; margin: 0 0 10px;
     white-space: pre-wrap;        /* CSS3 */
     white-space: -moz-pre-wrap; /* Firefox */
```

```
    white-space: -pre-wrap;      /* Opera <7 */
    white-space: -o-pre-wrap;    /* Opera 7 */
    word-wrap: break-word;       /* IE */}
button {width: 168px; height: 31px; cursor: pointer;
  margin-bottom: 10px;}
</style>
<script>

// Initialize the button click event handlers.
function init() {

<?php
  // Set button handlers based on logged-in status.
  if ($flgLoggedIn) {
    // User is logged in.
?>
  var buttonLogout = document.getElementById('logout');
  buttonLogout.addEventListener('click', launchLogout, false);
<?php
  } else {
    // User is not logged in.
?>
  var buttonLogin = document.getElementById('login');
  buttonLogin.addEventListener('click', launchLogin, false);
<?php } ?>
}

// Helper functions for button clicks.
function launchLogin() {
  window.open('<?php echo $auth_url;?>','_blank','height=550,
    width=400');
}
function launchLogout() {
  window.location.href = 'ppaccess_example.php?action=logout';
}

// Add the window load event listener.
window.addEventListener('load', init, false);

</script>
</head>
<body>
<?php
  if ($flgLoggedIn) {
    // User logged in.
?>
  <fieldset>
    <legend>PayPal Access - Logged In</legend>
    <div><button id="logout">Log Out</button></div>
  </fieldset>
  <fieldset>
    <legend>Profile</legend>
```

```php
    <ol>
      <li>Name: <?php echo $_SESSION['PROFILE']->name;?></li>
      <li>Email: <?php echo $_SESSION['PROFILE']->email;?></li>
      <li>Address:<br/>
        <?php echo $_SESSION['PROFILE']->address->street_address;?>
        <br/>
        <?php echo $_SESSION['PROFILE']->address->locality.", ".
                   $_SESSION['PROFILE']->address->region." ".
                   $_SESSION['PROFILE']->address->postal_code;?></li>
      <li>Country: <?php echo $_SESSION['PROFILE']->address->country;?>
      </li>
      <li>Language: <?php echo $_SESSION['PROFILE']->language;?></li>
      <li>Locale: <?php echo $_SESSION['PROFILE']->locale;?></li>
      <li>Zone: <?php echo $_SESSION['PROFILE']->zoneinfo;?></li>
      <li>User ID: <?php echo $_SESSION['PROFILE']->user_id;?></li>
    </ol>
  </fieldset>
  <fieldset>
    <legend>Token Info</legend>
    <ol>
      <li>Token Type: <?php echo $_SESSION['TOKEN']->token_type;?></li>
      <li>Expires: <?php echo $_SESSION['TOKEN']->expires_in;?></li>
      <li>Refresh Token:<br/>
        <?php echo $_SESSION['TOKEN']->refresh_token;?></li>
      <li>ID Token:<br/><?php echo $_SESSION['TOKEN']->id_token;?></li>
      <li>Access Token:<br/>
        <?php echo $_SESSION['TOKEN']->access_token;?></li>
    </ol>
  </fieldset>
<?php
  } else {
    // User not logged in.
?>
  <fieldset>
    <legend>PayPal Access - Not Logged In</legend>
    <div>
      <button id="login">
        <img src=
          "https://www.paypalobjects.com/en_US/Marketing/i/btn/
          login-with-paypal-button.png" />
      </button>
    </div>
  </fieldset>
<?php
  } // End check if user logged in.
?>
</body>
</html>
```

In the *ppaccess_example.php* page, the *auth.php* class file is included and the output will be based on whether or not the user is presently logged into the website. This is set with a simple session flag containing the token object that will be returned once the user logs in. In a production environment you can use your own method of validating whether or not the user is logged in. In the top code of the page there is also a check to determine if the user has selected to log out of the site, which simply *unsets* the session variable. This will allow you to test logging in and out multiple times using the PayPal Access service.

If the user is not logged in, the code will display on the page that the user is not logged in and provide an image button for logging in. It is recommended to use a link to the PayPal image for the button rather than storing the button on your site, as the image may be updated in the future. The link for the button image is here (*https://www.paypa lobjects.com/en_US/Marketing/i/btn/login-with-paypal-button.png*) and the current image is shown in Figure 2-21.

Figure 2-21. "Log in with PayPal Access" button

When the user clicks the button, a JavaScript event handler fires and executes the launchLogin function. This function opens a new window with the recommended dimensions of 550 pixels high and 400 pixels wide. The address URL provided to the window is dynamically generated through a request to the PayPal Access URL via a method in the PayPalAccess class, get_auth_url. The resulting window will present a login form for the user to enter her PayPal credentials in, as shown in Figure 2-22.

As expected, the browser window shows an authenticated and secure URL and the content states that the user is using her PayPal account information to log into your application. After the user enters her credentials and clicks "Log In," PayPal Access will validate the account and then present the user with a scope allowance screen, as shown in Figure 2-23.

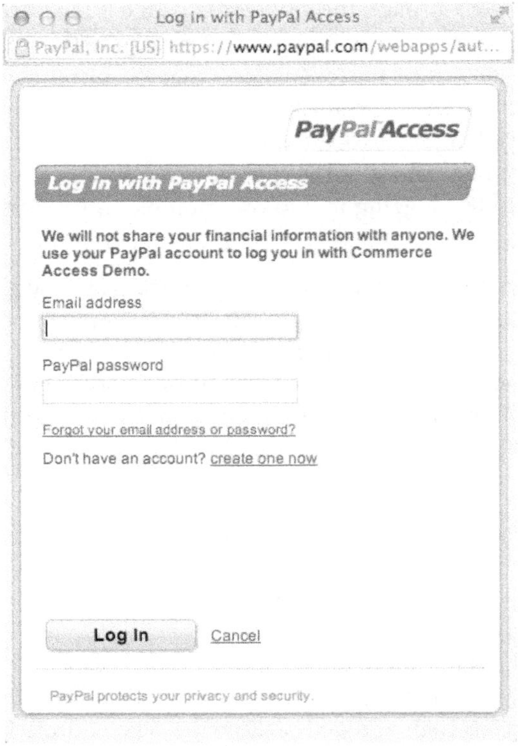

Figure 2-22. PayPal Access Login form

The allow access form confirms with the user that she is allowing PayPal to share the profile information requested with your website. It is important to note that this form is only displayed once to the user if she accepts. In subsequent logins the user is not asked to allow this sharing of information, since it has been shared in the past.

> Since PayPal Access is based on the user's PayPal account information, users can also manage which websites they want to share profile information with via their PayPal accounts. If a user desires, he can log into his PayPal account, go to "My Account Settings," and, under "Preferred Sites," not only see what is shared with a website but also remove his consent for sharing information with that website. If a user changes his mind about sharing his profile information with your site, a notice will be sent to your registered application's administration email address instructing the removal of any information that has been shared. If the user logs in via PayPal Access on your site in the future, he will be asked to allow the sharing of data once more.

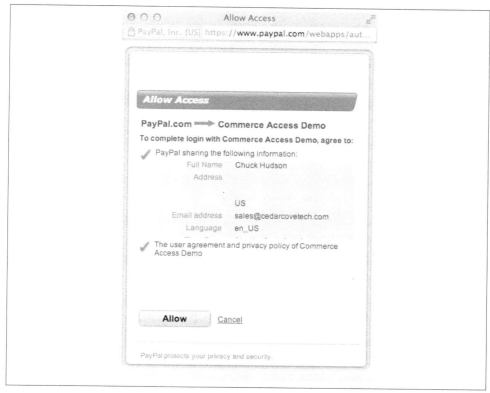

Figure 2-23. PayPal access scope sharing

Once the user allows the profile information to be shared, the window is closed and the user is returned to the return URL that was defined in the *auth.php* file. In this case the user is returned to *authReturn.php*, which is listed in Example 2-3.

Example 2-3. authReturn.php return URL page

```
<?php
/**********************************************
authReturn.php

This file checks the return from PayPal Access.
If the login was successful, the code retrieves
the token information and profile information.

Called by PayPal Access upon return.

Uses the auth.php PayPal Access library via
OpenID Connect found at:
https://github.com/jcleblanc/paypal-access.
```

```
**********************************************/

session_start();

// Require the auth library.
require_once('auth.php');

// Initialize a PayPalAccess instance.
$ppaccess = new PayPalAccess();

// If the code variable is present, returning from
// PayPal Access login.
if (isset($_GET['code'])){

  // Ask for a set of tokens from PayPal Access.
  $token = $ppaccess->get_access_token();

  // Check for a token retrieval error.
  if (!isset($token->error)) {

    // Save the token settings in the session for debugging.
    $_SESSION['TOKEN'] = $token;

    // Get the profile through PayPal Access using the
    // tokens retrieved.
    $profile = $ppaccess->get_profile();
    if (isset($profile)) {

      // Store the profile in the session for now.
      $_SESSION['PROFILE'] = $profile;
    }

    // End the session with PayPal Access.
    $ppaccess->end_session();

    // Echo out JavaScript to refresh the base window and close
    // this window.
    echo '<script>window.opener.location.href =
      "ppaccess_example.php";window.close();</script>';

  } else {
    // An error has occurred while acquiring the tokens.
    echo "Error: " . $token->error . " :: " .
      $token->error_description;
  }

// If the code parameter is not available, the user should be
// pushed to auth.
} else {

  // Handle case where there was an error during auth (e.g.,
```

```
// the user didn't log in, refused permissions, invalid_scope).
if (isset($_GET['error_uri'])){

  echo "You need to log in via PayPal Access.";

// If no error then need to push to PayPal Access.
} else {

  // Get auth URL and redirect user's browser to PayPal to log in.
  $url = $ppaccess->get_auth_url();
  header("Location: $url");
  }
}
?>
```

When loaded, the *authReturn.php* file will include the *auth.php* class and instantiate a PayPalAccess object. Next, the file will check if a code has been included in the query string. If included, the code signifies that the file has been called from the PayPal Access service after successful completion of the login process. To validate that this is an authentic OpenID Connect session, the page will request the access token from the PayPal Access service. If an error is returned, the particular error is displayed, but you can handle the error as needed and send the user to the PayPal Access authentication URL or return the user to the website without logging her in.

It is worth noting that the token returned by PayPal Access is not a single token, but a token object including various token properties and separate tokens. Example 2-4 shows the token object returned and its properties.

Example 2-4. Resulting token access object

```
[token_type] => Bearer
[expires_in] => 900
[refresh_token] => 18198637SA996854W
[id_token] => eyJ0eXAiOiJKV1QiLCJhbGciOiJIUzI1NiJ9.eyJhdWQiOiI3NzRh
YWVmOWEzMGY3NjhiMzIxNGJlNjAxOTM3OWU5YyIsImF1dGhfdGltZSI6MTM0OTAyNDM
5OCwiaXNzIjoiaHR0cHM6Ly93d3cucGF5cGFsLmNvbSIsInN1c3Npb25JbmRleCI6Ij
Q2NjE1NTNiNmM5MmIwMjI1NGFkZmJjNGQ5OTNkOTM4MTJmNmI4NjIiLCJpYXQiOjEzN
DkwMjQ0MDEsImV4cCI6Mjg4MDAsIm5vbmNlIjoiMTM0OTAyNDM4MjE4MjczNjc3MTgi
LCJ1c2VyX2lkIjoiaHR0cHM6Ly93d3cucGF5cGFsLmNvbS93ZWJhcHBzL2F1dGgvaWR
lbnRpdHkvdXNlci9zMzMN3TVpneVddLMVBLOFBRUWNDLTJzRDhMcks0T0VuWm55BUHFKZz
BwY2lRIn0=.9SSdbnDpPhAXgySQM8ViucU9VAe9iEXkM8LwkPwnSmg
[access_token]                                  =>
M9COMwk4EPbMeGNDBbXZM3dRv8aLRMy8lf5u4NEohLnE_dO6I_k2PnEndEXGfnhQD7-1Bg
```

In the token object, the type of the token is returned along with the number of seconds in which the access token will expire. In this case the token will expire in 900 seconds, or 15 minutes. For our example we will not be keeping the session open longer than is necessary to retrieve the tokens and profile information, but in some cases you may wish to do so. To keep the session open, you will need to use the refresh token to refresh the session on a regular basis. Refresh tokens are good for 8 hours. For more information on the tokens and refresh functions, see the OpenID Connect Integration for PayPal Access Getting Started Guide (*https://www.x.com/developers/paypal/documentation-tools/quick-start-guides/openid-connect-integration-paypal-access*).

Once the tokens have been retrieved by the `PayPalAccess` class instance, the example code requests the attributes of the user's profile through the `get_profile` method. If the profile attributes object is returned, the profile is stored in the `Session` object for convenience. At this point you can handle the information as you wish, perhaps storing it in a database or merging the data with other account information. The profile information will be stored in the `Session` object with the token object so that it can be easily displayed for debugging purposes.

After completing the profile request the code closes the OpenID Connect session, which ends the session with the PayPal Access service. At this point the tokens retrieved are no longer valid and cannot be used to make calls to the PayPal Access service. If you wanted to make subsequent calls to the service from other pages, you would want to keep the session open and keep the token data for the `PayPalAccess` class to use.

 In addition to this simple example of logging in, retrieving tokens, and accessing the profile attributes, a more complex example is available that allows for manually refreshing tokens and ending the session. This second example is available in the corresponding chapter code of the book's online code repository.

An example of the profile attributes object that is returned is shown in Example 2-5.

Example 2-5. Resulting profile object

```
address (
  [postal_code] => 92027
  [locality] => Atlanta
  [region] => GA
  [country] => US
  [street_address] => 218 Main St.
)
[language] => en_US
[verified] => true [locale] => en_US
[zoneinfo] => America/Los_Angeles
[name] => Charles Hudson
[email] => chudson@aduci.com
[user_id] => https://www.paypal.com/webapps/auth/identity/user/
  s33wMZgyWK1PK8PQQcC-2sD8LrK4OEnZnAPqJg0pcAQ
```

The properties in the JSON return include the profile information, email address, and physical address, as specified in the `scopes` attribute of the PayPal Access profile request in the *auth.php* file. Notice that the return also includes a `user_id` property. This is PayPal's unique ID for the user. You can use this ID to uniquely identify and match the user to your customer information, thus allowing you to merge the OpenID Connect profile information with your own.

When the OpenID Connect session is ended, the page refreshes the opening (parent) window's contents and closes the child window. When refreshed, the *ppaccess_ example.php* file recognizes that the user has logged in successfully and displays the profile information and token data that were stored in the session. In turn, you could then present customized product information based on the customer's profile information or linked customer information from your database.

See Also

PayPal Access Overview (*https://www.x.com/developers/paypal/products/paypal-access*)

Getting to Know PayPal Access (*http://bit.ly/UaR897*)

OpenID Connect Integration for PayPal Access Getting Started Guide (*http://bit.ly/ WokenN*)

2.3. Presenting Similar Items

Opportunity

Presenting a product to a customer via a web store is fairly straightforward, and the product description can contain a wide range of information. However, if the product does not match the users' needs exactly, they may leave your website and seek out another vendor, resulting in the potential loss of a sales and customers.

Solution

Even though a website may not carry the exact match for an item desired by a customer, there is the potential to assist the customer and start a relationship by showing similar items from eBay as an up-sell or cross-sell opportunity. eBay provides a Merchandising API that can be used to retrieve eBay listings similar to a particular item. These items can be displayed on a vendor's site with a link to the eBay items for purchase. Not only can the customer end up purchasing the desired product and feeling good about finding the item on the website visited, but the website can potentially receive affiliate fees for leading the customer to eBay.

Discussion

The eBay Merchandising API (*http://bit.ly/ZgMaLY*) contains five calls that provide retrieval methods for items and recommendations from eBay:

`getMostWatchedItems`

    Retrieves items with the highest watch counts

`getRelatedCategoryItems`

    Retrieves items related to a specific category or item

`getSimilarItems`

    Retrieves items similar to a provided item

`getTopSellingProducts`

    Retrieves the top-selling items by sales rank

`getVersion`

    Retrieves the version of the Merchandising API service

This example will call `getSimilarItems` (*http://bit.ly/VOaOf2*) to retrieve a list of 10 similar "Buy It Now" items on eBay based on a provided eBay item ID. The item ID provided in the request to `getSimilarItems` must be for an item on eBay that has expired within the past two weeks. The service will take the item ID passed in with the call and return an array of similar items and their various properties, including the item image, title, price, and viewing link. Figure 2-24 shows the resulting display of items if an item ID was passed in for an iPhone 5.

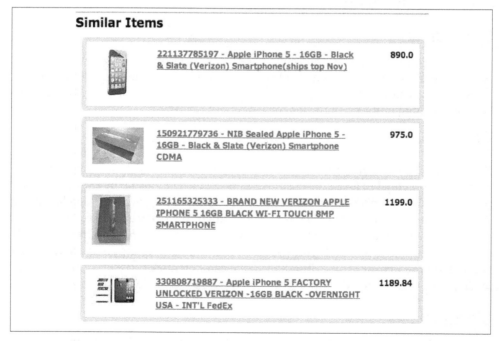

Figure 2-24. Sample eBay Similar Items list

The first step to running this example is to create a new application in the developer.ebay.com site. When the application is created a set of keys will be provided, including an application ID (AppID) that will be used as an identifier for your app for requests to the eBay servers. To create your application ID, log into the developer.ebay.com site and go to the "My Account" menu option.

Once you have your AppID, enter the string into the *merchandisingConstants.php* API_KEY constant, replacing the value of the *<YOUR_API_KEY>* field as seen in Example 2-6. The *merchandisingConstants.php* file will be used to load constants used in making the getSimilarItems call. You will notice that besides the API key, the endpoints are defined for the service, the service version, the eBay site to use for the items, and the format of the request and response data for the call. In this example the data format for the request and response will be JSON, but you could use name/value pairs or XML formats depending on your specific needs. To learn more about structuring requests with other data formats, see the eBay Merchandising API "Making an API Call" (*http://bit.ly/UaRvAu*) document.

Example 2-6. merchandisingConstants.php constants file

```php
<?php
/*********************************************
merchandisingConstants.php

Constants used for Merchandising API calls.

*********************************************/

// eBay developer API key for production
DEFINE("API_KEY","<YOUR_API_KEY>");

// eBay Merchandising API constants
DEFINE("MERCHANDISING_API_ENDPOINT",
  "http://svcs.ebay.com/MerchandisingService");
DEFINE("MERCHANDISING_SANDBOX_API_ENDPOINT",
  "http://svcs.sandbox.ebay.com/MerchandisingService");
DEFINE("MERCHANDISING_API_VERSION","1.1.0");

// eBay site to use - 0 = United States
DEFINE("GLOBAL_ID","EBAY-US");

// encoding format - JSON
DEFINE("REQUEST_ENCODING","JSON");
DEFINE("RESPONSE_ENCODING","JSON");
?>
```

The main file for this example is *getSimilarItems.php*, shown in Example 2-7. This file will include the *merchandisingConstants.php* file, create the JSON request structure, execute the curl call, and process the results. Depending on whether your application is registered for the eBay sandbox or production environments, the proper endpoint will need to be used in the *getSimilarItems.php* file. In Example 2-7 the production endpoint for the Merchandising API is used. If instead your app is using the sandbox, the sandbox endpoint will be needed. To change the endpoint, change the constant value provided to the `curl_init` method in the *getSimilarItems.php* file from `MERCHANDIS ING_API_ENDPOINT` to `MERCHANDISING_SANDBOX_API_ENDPOINT`.

For the JSON request, three variables are used: `itemId`, `listingType`, and `max Results`. The `itemId` is the only field that is required, but the `listingType` variable allows filtering of the type of listings returned and the `maxResults` variable provides a limit on the number of items returned. In this case the listings will be limited to `Fixed PriceItem` and a maximum of 10 items will be returned.

> In addition to these optional fields, the `getSimilarItems` call can accept an affiliate block of information. As a third party executing the `getSimilarItems` call, you can include a set of IDs corresponding to an eBay affiliate account. The `getSimilarItems` call will then wrap the view item URL and the product URL with the affiliate information. If a customer from your site then opens either URL, you will have the opportunity to receive affiliate revenue from purchases made on the eBay site.

The `itemId` value will need to be updated to a recent item for you to execute this example properly, since the item needs to be recently expired on eBay (within the last two weeks). To retrieve an item ID you can use one of the eBay Finding APIs to search based on keyword, or for demonstration purposes a simple search of the eBay site in your browser will expose the item ID, titled *item number* on any item listing.

Example 2-7. getSimilarItems.php item retrieval and display

```php
<?php
/**********************************************
getSimilarItems.php

Uses getSimilarItems of the eBay Merchandising
API to display 10 items similar to a recently
closed item on eBay, given the item ID.

Requires the merchandisingConstants.php file.
**********************************************/

// Include our Merchandising API constants.
require_once 'merchandisingConstants.php';

// Create the JSON request variables.
// Replace the itemId with a recently (within
// 2 weeks) completed eBay item ID.
$jsonRequest = '{
```

```php
  "itemId":"170923268700",
  "listingType":"FixedPriceItem",
  "maxResults":"10"
}';

// Define the header array for the Merchandising API call.
$headers = array(
  'X-EBAY-SOA-OPERATION-NAME:getSimilarItems',
  'X-EBAY-SOA-SERVICE-NAME:MerchandisingService',
  'X-EBAY-SOA-SERVICE-VERSION:'.MERCHANDISING_API_VERSION,
  'EBAY-SOA-CONSUMER-ID:'.API_KEY,
  'X-EBAY-SOA-GLOBAL-ID:'.GLOBAL_ID,
  'X-EBAY-SOA-REQUEST-DATA-FORMAT:'.REQUEST_ENCODING,
  'X-EBAY-SOA-RESPONSE-DATA-FORMAT:'.RESPONSE_ENCODING
);

// Initialize the curl session.
$session  = curl_init(MERCHANDISING_API_ENDPOINT);

// Set the curl HTTP POST options with the JSON request.
curl_setopt($session, CURLOPT_HTTPHEADER, $headers);
curl_setopt($session, CURLOPT_POST, true);
curl_setopt($session, CURLOPT_POSTFIELDS, $jsonRequest);
curl_setopt($session, CURLOPT_RETURNTRANSFER, true);

// Execute the curl request.
$responseJSON = curl_exec($session);

// Close the curl session.
curl_close($session);
?>

<!DOCTYPE html>
<html>
<head>
<meta charset="UTF-8" />
<title>2-4 Presenting Similar Items</title>
<style>
body {background: #fff; color: #000;
  font: normal 62.5%/1.5 tahoma, verdana, sans-serif;}
* {margin: 0; padding: 0;}
div.item {font-size: 1.3em; font-weight: bold; border: 7px solid #ccc;
  border-radius: 5px; padding: 10px; margin: 10px; width: 500px;
  vertical-align: top;}
div.itemImage {float: left; display: block; width: 100px;}
div.itemTitle {float: left; display: block; width: 320px;}
div.itemPrice {float: right;}
</style>
</head>
<body>

<?php
// Convert the JSON to a PHP object.
```

```php
$objResponse = json_decode($responseJSON);

// Set the call ack response value.
$ack = $objResponse->getSimilarItemsResponse->ack;

// Check if the call to the Merchandising API was successful.
if ($ack == "Success") {

  // Get a reference to the array of items.
  $items =
    $objResponse->getSimilarItemsResponse->itemRecommendations->item;

  // Loop through the items and display.
  echo '<H1>Similar Items</H1>';
  foreach ($items as $item) {
    // Display the image, title, item ID, and price.
    echo '<div class="item" style="overflow:hidden">';
    echo '<div class="itemImage"><img src="'.$item->imageURL.'"/>
      </div>';
    echo '<div class="itemTitle"><a href="'.$item->viewItemURL.'">
      '.$item->itemId." - ".$item>title.'</a></div>';
    echo '<div class="itemPrice">'.$item->buyItNowPrice->
      __value__.'</div>';
    echo '</div>';
  }
} else {
  // Call to Merchandising API failed.
  $errors = $objResponse->getSimilarItemsResponse->errorMessage->error;

  // Display errors.
  echo '<H1>'.count($errors).' Error(s)</H1>';
  foreach ($errors as $error) {
    echo "Error Id " . $error->errorId . " :: " . $error->message .
      "<br/>";
  }
}
?>

</body>
</html>
```

After the call to getSimilarItems is complete, a JSON block will be returned containing either an error condition or a success. Figure 2-25 shows a sample JSON response object containing several items. The code in the display portion of the HTML will first check whether the ack field has a return code that is equal to Success, designating that the call was successful. Otherwise, the error handling at the bottom of the page will be triggered.

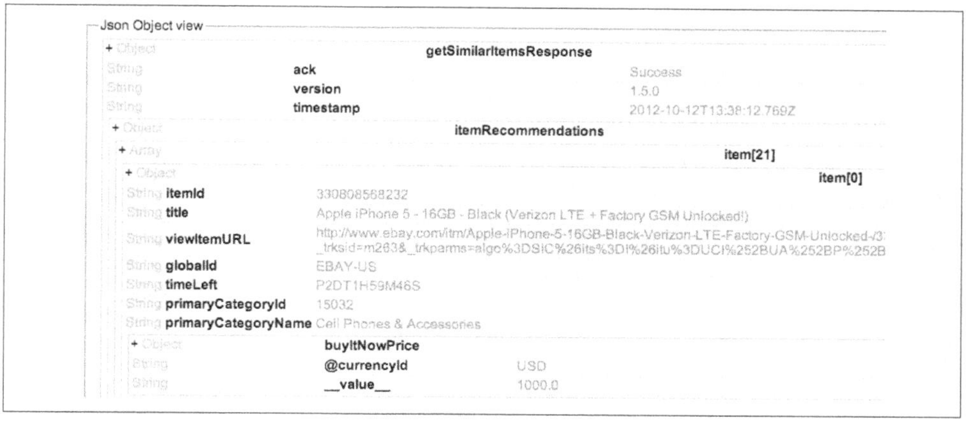

Figure 2-25. Sample JSON items returned

If the call was successful, a pointer to the item array in the JSON object will be set and the array of items will be looped through, displaying the image, title, view link, and current "Buy It Now" price. There are other fields that may be of interest in your solution, including the time remaining, shipping costs, and category ID.

If an error is returned, the ack property will be set to Failure. This designates that the call to getSimilarItems was received by the eBay services but not successfully executed. In Figure 2-26 a sample JSON error object is shown, displaying an "Invalid Item ID" error.

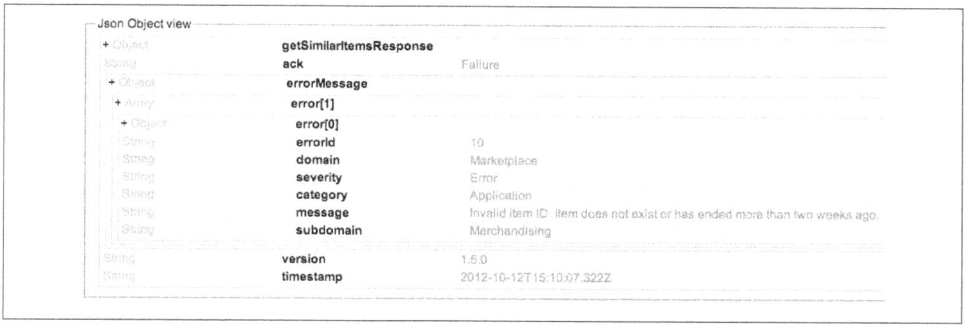

Figure 2-26. Sample error with invalid item ID

This example has shown how easy it is to leverage the eBay Merchandising API to show items similar to an item of your choosing. This could be integrated into a vendor website as an up-sell opportunity or even a cross-sell opportunity, depending on the purpose of the website. As well, the other Merchandising API calls may be of benefit to populate popular items via the top-selling and most-watched services available.

See Also

eBay Merchandising API (*https://www.x.com/developers/ebay/products/merchandising-api*)

eBay Merchandising API – Making an API Call (*http://developer.ebay.com/DevZone/merchandising/docs/Concepts/MerchandisingAPI_FormatOverview.html*)

eBay Merchandising API getSimilarItems call reference (*http://developer.ebay.com/DevZone/merchandising/docs/CallRef/getSimilarItems.html*)

2.4. Conclusion

This chapter has exposed some of the exciting technologies that can be integrated into your commerce site, whether your site is based on Magento or a homegrown storefront. The first recipe touched upon integrating social content into product presentation by leveraging a social framework. The addition of the social element to the commerce lifecycle can be extremely powerful in moving people to the next step: purchasing.

In the second recipe we looked briefly at incorporating OpenID Connect with PayPal Access and Identity services, not only to minimize the work needed for incorporating single sign-on but also to retrieve profile information. Visitors can now sign in with just their PayPal credentials in a secure and trusted interface. At the same time, risk is minimized by not having to store visitor login credentials, and beneficial profile data can be provided. This profile data can then be used in a number of ways, including for dynamic and customized product presentation.

The final recipe looked at presenting products similar to the one being shown to the consumer via eBay's Merchandising API to cross- or up-sell the consumer on goods that may not be in your product catalog. With this method, you can strengthen your relationship with the consumer by making applicable recommendations.

Hopefully you have seen just how powerful these enhancements and integrations into your commerce site can be. Now that the consumer has found the product he wants to purchase and been presented with the information necessary for making the purchasing decision, we can focus on streamlining the purchase process. This is the focus of the next chapter and the next stage of the commerce lifecycle.

CHAPTER 3

Enhancing the Payment Experience

The purchase stage in the simplified commerce lifecycle (Figure 3-1) is the final hurdle before a vendor is able to establish the buyer/seller relationship with a potential customer. Several opportunities exist in this stage to enhance the process, for example, by shortening the payment process and changing the process from a series of necessary steps to a positive user experience. If the process is complex, confusing, or just plain troublesome for a user, there is the potential to not only irritate the user but also lose the sale and have the commerce lifecycle end.

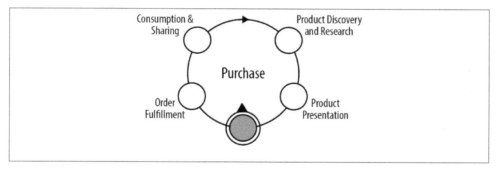

Figure 3-1. Simplified commerce lifecycle—stage 3

In this chapter the examples will focus on streamlining the purchase and payment process, while making it an experience that can be both rewarding and positively memorable for the customer. If successful, this step can contribute to the likelihood of a customer returning to the site and becoming a member of the seller's loyal customer base.

Our first example will show how you can encourage visitors to complete the purchase process on your site through individualized coupons generated in a Magento storefront. This example will include extending the Magento REST API to allow for integration of these coupon codes into marketing services and other business systems. For those businesses where subsequent purchases are key, the second example will show the use of preapproval payments, whereby a customer can authorize future payments with one click. Finally, this chapter's last example will examine the use of parallel payments via the PayPal Adaptive Payments API to create a positive emotional association with the purchase by providing a charity donation option during the checkout process.

The overall goals for this stage in the lifecycle are to use APIs to expedite the purchase process, make it something that has positive ties for the consumer, and keep customers focused on completing the purchase.

3.1. Autogenerating Coupons with Magento

Opportunity

Couponing has become a wide social phenomenon, both in the brick-and-mortar store checkout line and online. Coupon codes can be emailed or mailed to users, who can then input them upon checkout in an online shopping experience, resulting in a more rewarding experience for the consumer and, if handled correctly, providing important marketing information for the vendor.

Solution

In release 1.7 of the Magento Community Edition a new method of creating coupon codes was added, titled "Auto Generation." With this method, several coupon codes can be generated at one time. Individual coupon codes can then be distributed to customers, and vendors are able to see which codes have been used. However, doing this manually for large amounts of customers can be time-consuming and labor-intensive. This recipe will show how to leverage the autogenerated coupon codes through an extended REST API, which can be called by an outside program to automatically generate a number of codes for distribution. In this manner, as an example, you could email your top 100 customers an individual coupon code quite easily.

Discussion

The Auto Generation option in Magento 1.7 allows Magento to automatically generate one or more coupon codes for a particular Shopping Cart Price Rule. Magento allows you to export these codes, but it would be nice to dynamically call a REST-based API to generate a series of codes that can then automatically be put into an email campaign or other promotion vehicle. For a brief introduction to the Magento REST interface, see the "Introduction to REST API" (*http://bit.ly/V3DIHo*) document on the Magento website. To illustrate extending this REST API and adding a web service for generating and retrieving coupon codes, this example will walk through four main steps:

1. Setting up an autogenerating coupon rule in Magento
2. Adding a new REST-based API extension
3. Creating a user for the OAuth access to the new service
4. Testing the web service from an external web page

Setting up the autogenerating coupon rule

To create a new autogenerating coupon code rule, you will need to log into your Magento Admin Panel and select "Shopping Cart Price Rules" under the Promotions menu option (Figure 3-2).

Figure 3-2. Creating a new shopping cart price rule

The Shopping Cart Price Rules screen will list any rules you have currently for your shopping cart, including any discounts or coupons. To create a new rule, select "Add New Rule" in the top-right corner. This will open the "New Rule" screen, which will have a form for adding the new rule, conditions, actions, and labels. If you need more information on the various form fields, you can find documentation on creating coupon codes in the Magento Knowledge Base (*http://bit.ly/UaRHzy*). The parts that are important for autogeneration of codes are the fields *Coupon* and *Coupon Code*. To have the rule use autogeneration, change the *Coupon* value to "Specific Coupon," which will display the "Use Auto Generation" option (Figure 3-3). Check the checkbox next to "Use Auto Generation," fill out the rest of your rule, and click "Save."

Figure 3-3. Creating a rule with coupon autogeneration

Now that the rule is in place, you can manually generate new coupon codes by selecting the rule from the list and clicking on "Manage Coupon Codes" in the Shopping Cart Price Rule detail screen, as seen in Figure 3-4.

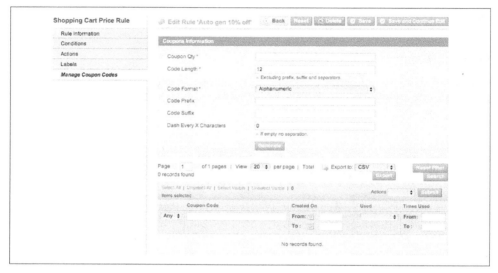

Figure 3-4. Manually generating new coupon codes

The "Coupons Information" form allows you to designate the number of coupons, the length of the coupon code, its format, and some other optional properties. When you click "Generate," the coupon codes will be generated and displayed in the list at the bottom of the screen.

The Magento system will track which coupon codes have been used in the list of coupon codes under the "Manage Coupon Codes" section. The coupon codes can be exported to CSV (i.e., as a comma-separated values file), but we will extend Magento so that we can generate and retrieve new codes dynamically by calling a new REST-based API that we will create.

Setting up the extended REST API

In several cases you may have a need to create and pull coupon codes for incorporation into another application, such as an email-marketing tool, or to display on your site to individual users. Currently the Magento API does not provide a web service that provides for the autogeneration of coupon codes. However, the REST-based API architecture that Magento has released is both flexible and extensible. Based on this framework, we will add a new web service that will take four parameters:

1. The *rule ID* that we want to create codes for
2. The *quantity* of codes to create
3. The *length* that each code should be
4. The *format* for the generation of the codes

The web service will use these parameters to instantiate the underlying Mage sales rule (`salesrule/rule`) coupon code generator and create a pool of new codes. These codes will be added to the system and returned to the caller via a JSON string.

To create a REST-based extension API in Magento, we'll define a new module with a specified directory structure and five required files:

1. *<module>.xml*
2. *config.xml*
3. *api.xml*
4. *api2.xml*
5. *V1.php*

The first thing we need to do is tell Magento that we are adding a new module to the system. This is done with a *<module>.xml* file, which describes the new module and where the module definition can be found in the system. In this case we will name our module `CommerceBook_AutoGen`, so the file will be named *CommerceBook_Auto Gen.xml* and should mirror Example 3-1. The important sections in the module definition are the module name (`<CommerceBook_AutoGen>`) and `<codePool>` tags, which inform Magento as to the location of the model for this module.

Example 3-1. Module definition XML file

```xml
<?xml version="1.0"?>
<config>
  <modules>
    <CommerceBook_AutoGen>
      <active>true</active>
      <codePool>community</codePool>
    </CommerceBook_AutoGen>
  </modules>
</config>
```

Once created, the file should be placed in the *app/etc/modules* directory, as seen in Figure 3-5.

Figure 3-5. Location of module definition XML file

Now that Magento knows about the new module, the module directory structure and files need to be added in the "community" code area under *app/code/community*. It is important to make sure that the naming and directory structure are kept the same as what is defined here, as Magento uses this structure to configure the module and execute the module logic. The file and directory structure will mimic the normal Magento REST-based APIs: there will be an *etc* folder for the configuration of the REST-based service and a *Model* folder for the model directory structure. Figure 3-6 shows the directory structure that should be created and the locations of the XML configuration files and the web service file, *V1.php*.

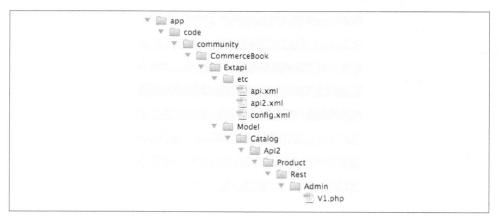

Figure 3-6. REST-based module API directory structure

In Example 3-2 the module and model are defined in the *config.xml* file.

Example 3-2. config.xml model definition file

```xml
<?xml version="1.0"?>
<config>
  <modules>
```

```
<CommerceBook_AutoGen>
  <version>0.1.0</version>
</CommerceBook_AutoGen>
</modules>
<global>
  <models>
    <autogen>
      <class>CommerceBook_AutoGen_Model</class>
    </autogen>
  </models>
</global>
</config>
```

 By default Magento has *system caching* turned on, including caching of modules and web service information. If you are changing the module directory structure or configuration XML files, you will need to either turn off the caching temporarily while development occurs or flush the cache each time that you update the files by going into the System → Cache Management interface (Figure 3-7). If you receive errors doing development such as "Route to resource not found," you should clear your cache to try and rectify the issue.

Figure 3-7. Magento cache management

Now that Magento has the correct structure for the module, the API XML configuration files that provide the location of the specific service and service characteristics such as privileges and routes can be added. In the *api.xml* file the service is defined with the appropriate method, faults, and access control list (acl), as shown in Example 3-3.

Example 3-3. api.xml web service definition

```
<?xml version="1.0"?>
<config>
  <api>
    <resources>
      <autogen_catalog translate="title" module="autogen">
        <model>autogen/catalog_api2</model>
```

```
              <title>autogen catalog API</title>
              <acl>extcatalog</acl>
              <methods>
                <list translate="title" module="autogen">
                  <title>Retrieve Coupon Codes</title>
                  <method>retrieve</method>
                  <acl>extcatalog/info</acl>
                </list>
              </methods>
              <faults module="autogen">
                <data_invalid>
                  <code>100</code>
                  <message>Invalid Request.</message>
                </data_invalid>
              </faults>
            </autogen_catalog>
          </resources>
          <v2>
            <resources_function_prefix>
              <autogen_catalog>autogen_catalog</autogen_catalog>
            </resources_function_prefix>
          </v2>
          <acl>
            <resources>
              <autogen_catalog translate="title" module="autogen">
                <title>catalog</title>
                <sort_order>3</sort_order>
                <info translate="title" module="autogen">
                  <title>Create and retrieve coupon codes</title>
                </info>
              </autogen_catalog>
            </resources>
          </acl>
      </api>
</config>
```

The *api2.xml* file in Example 3-4 defines the resources and route information. The route
XML definition is important for telling the system where to find the specific service
code file.

Example 3-4. api2.xml web service definition

```
<?xml version="1.0"?>
<config>
  <api2>
    <resource_groups>
      <autogen translate="title" module="api2">
        <title>CommerceBook API calls</title>
        <sort_order>30</sort_order>
        <children>
          <autogen_product translate="title" module="api2">
            <title>Product</title>
```

```
            <sort_order>50</sort_order>
          </autogen_product>
        </children>
      </autogen>
    </resource_groups>
    <resources>
      <autogenproducts translate="title" module="api2">
        <group>autogen_product</group>
        <model>autogen/catalog_api2_product</model>
        <working_model>autogen/catalog_api2_product</working_model>
        <title>Coupon Code Auto Generation</title>
        <sort_order>10</sort_order>
        <privileges>
          <admin>
            <retrieve>1</retrieve>
          </admin>
        </privileges>
        <routes>
          <route_entity_retrieve>
            <route>/commercebook/products/retrieve</route>
            <action_type>entity</action_type>
          </route_entity_retrieve>
        </routes>
        <versions>1</versions>
      </autogenproducts>
    </resources>
  </api2>
</config>
```

The last step in creating the web service is to drop the actual functional logic into the module. The PHP logic file should be named *V1.php*, to follow the Magento naming scheme, and will extend the `Mage_Api2_Model_Resource` class. Inside the file a protected function is added for `_retrieve`, which Magento will automatically map to the GET HTTP call action.

> Magento uses four "verbs" for accessing resources via the REST-based API (GET, POST, PUT, and DELETE) and automatically maps each to a corresponding function: GET → `_retrieve`, POST → `_create`, PUT → `_update`, and DELETE → `_delete`.

In the `_retrieve` function the code will consume the parameters passed to the call by using the `getRequest` method to get the request object, followed by the `getParams` method to access each parameter. The code will then load the specific shopping cart price rule requested and create an instance of the `CouponMassGenerator` object. The parameters will be passed to the generator, which will validate the parameters passed and generate the requested codes.

Since the Magento autogeneration coupon code objects are fairly new, there is not yet a method for easily retrieving the coupon codes that were added. However, there is a call to get all the coupon codes for a rule, and conveniently, the codes will be listed in the order in which they were generated. To get the list of added codes, the file will take note of the number of codes generated and then "slice" the array of coupon code objects. The file will loop through the resulting list and retrieve each coupon code from the coupon objects. The code listing for *V1.php* is in Example 3-5.

Example 3-5. V1.php REST web service

```php
<?php
/* Extended AutoCoupon api
 *
 * @category    CommerceBook
 * @package     CommerceBook_AutoGen
 * @author      Chuck Hudson
*/

class CommerceBook_AutoGen_Model_Catalog_Api2_Product_Rest_Admin_V1
  extends Mage_Api2_Model_Resource {

  /**
   * Add one or more sub-coupons to an established rule
   *
   * @param int $rule_id
   * @param int $qty
   * @param int $length
   * @param string $format
   *
   * @return JSON-encoded array of new coupon codes
   */

  protected function _retrieve() {

    // Retrieve the Request object.
    $params = $this->getRequest();

    $rule_id = $params->getParam('rule_id');
    $qty = $params->getParam('qty');
    $length = $params->getParam('length');
    $format = $params->getParam('format');

    // Set the passed-in arguments.
    $data['rule_id'] = $rule_id;
    $data['qty']     = $qty;
    $data['length']  = $length;

    /* Set the format of the coupon codes. Possible formats:
        alphanum    Alphanumeric
        alpha       Alphabetical
        num         Numeric
```

```
*/
$data['format']   = $format;

// Load the selected rule.
$rule = Mage::getModel('salesrule/rule')->load($rule_id);

// Reference the MassGenerator on this rule.
$generator = $rule->getCouponMassGenerator();

// Validate the generator.
if (!$generator->validateData($data)) {
  $result['error'] = Mage::helper('salesrule')->__('Not valid data
    provided');
} else {

  // Set the data for the generator.
  $generator->setData($data);

  // Generate the pool of coupon codes for the rule.
  $generator->generatePool();

  // Get the number of codes created.
  $generated = $generator->getGeneratedCount();
}

// Retrieve all the coupons under this rule.
$coupons = $rule->getCoupons();

// *** Trim reset index to 0.
$coupons = array_slice($coupons, count($coupons)-$generated);

// Set up our return array.
$coupon_codes = array();

// Loop through and grab the last qty codes.
for ($i=0; $i<count($coupons); $i++) {
  $coupon_codes[$i] = $coupons[$i]->code;
}

// Return the array of coupon code objects.
return json_encode(array('codes'=>$coupon_codes));
  }
}
?>
```

Configuring the REST OAuth user

To allow an outside request to the new web service, an OAuth user will need to be
authorized for the REST call. In Magento this is done under the System → Web Services
section, as seen in Figure 3-8.

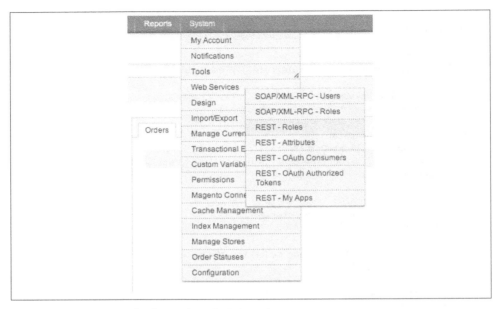

Figure 3-8. Location of web service administration

First, a new role is needed for accessing the web service. To add a role, select the "REST – Roles" option from the System → Web Services menu. Click "Add Admin Role," and add a role name. Then, in the "Roles Resources" section of the "Role API Resources" screen, select the "CommerceBook API calls" checkbox as shown in Figure 3-9. After adding the resources, click "Save Role."

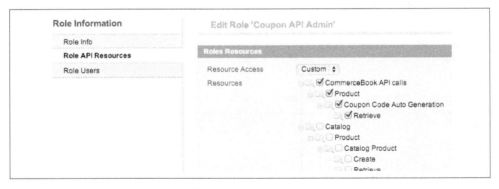

Figure 3-9. REST role creation with resources

Next, to acquire a consumer key and secret, you'll need to add an OAuth consumer. The page making the OAuth call in the next section will require these credentials. To add an

OAuth consumer in Magento, go to System → Web Services → REST – OAuth Consumers and click "Add New." A form will be provided, as shown in Figure 3-10. Add a consumer name and copy the key and secret provided so that these can be added into the calling page in the next section. Save the OAuth consumer information form.

Figure 3-10. OAuth consumer information form

The web service is now ready to be tested with the OAuth consumer.

Testing the new extended REST API

To test the new extended REST service call, you'll use a PHP page named *rest_test.php*. The page will make an OAuth version 1a (Magento's supported OAuth version) call for authorization and then make a GET request, sending the specific parameters across to the call. To make the OAuth call this example will use the OAuth *pecl* extension (*http://www.pecl.php.net*). You can verify that the system from which you are running the test call has the extension installed by running phpinfo and checking for the OAuth section, as shown in Figure 3-11.

OAuth	
OAuth support	**enabled**
PLAINTEXT support	enabled
RSA-SHA1 support	enabled
HMAC-SHA1 support	enabled
Request engine support	php_streams, curl
source version	$Id: oauth.c 313600 2011-07-22 16:48:24Z jawed $
version	1.2.2

Figure 3-11. OAuth installation verification

In the test call page (shown in Example 3-6), you'll need to add the consumerKey and consumerSecret acquired in the last section. Replace the appropriate fields at the top of the file with your generated consumer key and secret. Once the OAuth client is set up, the code will define the data to be passed in the $ruleData array. The data should include the rule ID (listed next to the rule in the rule list in the Magento Admin Panel), the number of codes desired, the length of the codes, and the format to be used. The format of coupon codes can be alphanumeric, alphabetical, or numeric. The array of parameters is then passed in the fetch command with the resourceUrl for the web service call.

Example 3-6. rest_test.php extended API test page

```php
<?php
/***********************************************************
rest_test.php

Test PHP file for calling our newly extended REST API auto-
genned coupon code web service, which will return a list of
coupon codes, given a particular rule ID, quantity, length,
and format for the codes.


***********************************************************/

// Set the key and secret for the authorized REST user.
$consumerKey = '<YOUR_CONSUMER_KEY>';
$consumerSecret = '<YOUR_CONSUMER_SECRET>';

// Set the callback URL for handling the results.
$callbackUrl = "http://apiris.com/rest_test.php";

// Set the applicable URLs for your Magento installation.
$temporaryCredentialsRequestUrl =
  "http://apiris.com/oauth/initiate?oauth_callback=" .
  urlencode($callbackUrl);
$adminAuthorizationUrl = 'http://apiris.com/admin/oauth_authorize';
$accessTokenRequestUrl = 'http://apiris.com/oauth/token';
$apiUrl = 'http://apiris.com/api/rest';

session_start();

if (!isset($_GET['oauth_token']) && isset($_SESSION['state']) &&
    $_SESSION['state'] == 1) {
  $_SESSION['state'] = 0;
}
try {
  $authType = ($_SESSION['state'] == 2) ?
    OAUTH_AUTH_TYPE_AUTHORIZATION : OAUTH_AUTH_TYPE_URI;
  $oauthClient = new OAuth($consumerKey, $consumerSecret,
    OAUTH_SIG_METHOD_HMACSHA1, $authType);
  $oauthClient->enableDebug();

  if (!isset($_GET['oauth_token']) && !$_SESSION['state']) {
    $requestToken =
      $oauthClient->getRequestToken($temporaryCredentialsRequestUrl);
    $_SESSION['secret'] = $requestToken['oauth_token_secret'];
    $_SESSION['state'] = 1;
```

```php
  header('Location: ' . $adminAuthorizationUrl . '?oauth_token=' .
    $requestToken['oauth_token']);
  exit;
} else if ($_SESSION['state'] == 1) {
  $oauthClient->setToken($_GET['oauth_token'], $_SESSION['secret']);
  $accessToken =
    $oauthClient->getAccessToken($accessTokenRequestUrl);
  $_SESSION['state'] = 2;
  $_SESSION['token'] = $accessToken['oauth_token'];
  $_SESSION['secret'] = $accessToken['oauth_token_secret'];
  header('Location: ' . $callbackUrl);
  exit;
} else {
  // We have the OAuth client and token; now let's make the API call.
  $oauthClient->setToken($_SESSION['token'], $_SESSION['secret']);
  $resourceUrl = "$apiUrl/products";

  // Set the array of params to send with the request.
  $ruleData = array();
  $ruleData['rule_id'] = 1;        // Coupon rule ID.
  $ruleData['qty'] = 10;           // Number of codes to create.
  $ruleData['length'] = 7;         // Length of each code.
  $ruleData['format'] = "alphanum"; // Set alphanumeric for format.
  /* Options for format include:
      alphanum   Alphanumeric
      alpha      Alphabetical
      num        Numeric */

  // Set and call the REST URL with the data array passed.
  $resourceUrl = "$apiUrl/commercebook/products/retrieve";
  $oauthClient->fetch($resourceUrl,$ruleData);

  // Get and decode the response from the call.
  // TODO: Should add any error handling necessary.
  $codeList = $oauthClient->getLastResponse();

  // Modify response, stripping slashes and extra double quotes.
  $strCodeList = stripslashes($codeList);
  $strCodeList = substr($strCodeList, 1, strlen($strCodeList) - 2);

  // Decode the JSON string.
  $newCodesObj = json_decode($strCodeList);

  // Create an array of the new codes generated.
  $arrNewCodes = $newCodesObj->codes;

  /* Display the newly created codes for debug; you could instead
    include them in an email, store them in a database, etc.*/
  echo "The codes created are:<br/>";
  foreach ($arrNewCodes as $newCode) {
    echo " --> " . $newCode . "<br/>";
  }
```

```
    }
} catch (OAuthException $e) {
    print_r($e);
}
?>
```

Once the call to the web service has completed, the returned JSON string is parsed and the test page loops through the array of new codes created, displaying each as in Figure 3-12.

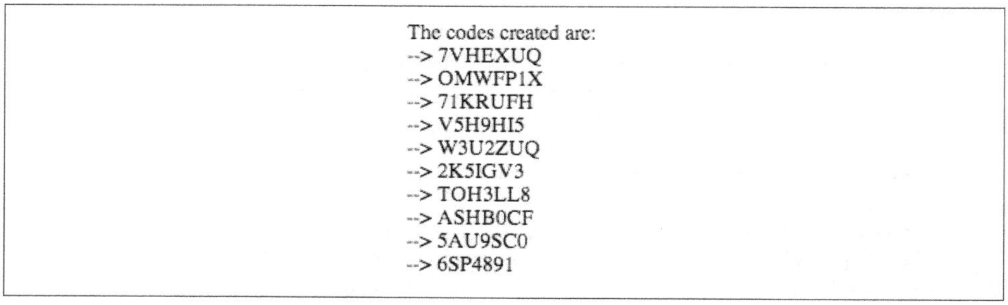

The codes created are:
--> 7VHEXUQ
--> OMWFP1X
--> 71KRUFH
--> V5H9HI5
--> W3U2ZUQ
--> 2K5IGV3
--> TOH3LL8
--> ASHB0CF
--> 5AU9SC0
--> 6SP4891

Figure 3-12. Resulting coupon codes from REST API call

To verify the codes, open the rule in the Magento Admin Panel and select the "Manage Coupon Codes" option. The new coupon codes should be included in the list of codes, similar to Figure 3-13.

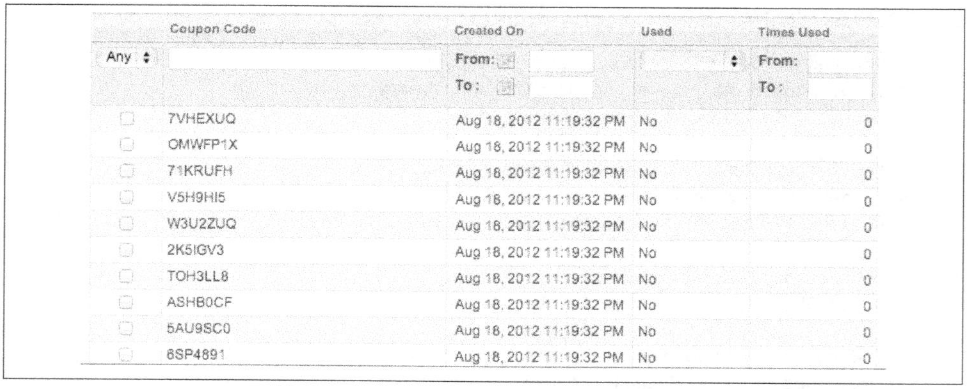

	Coupon Code	Created On	Used	Times Used
Any ⬍		From:	⬍	From:
		To:		To:
☐	7VHEXUQ	Aug 18, 2012 11:19:32 PM	No	0
☐	OMWFP1X	Aug 18, 2012 11:19:32 PM	No	0
☐	71KRUFH	Aug 18, 2012 11:19:32 PM	No	0
☐	V5H9HI5	Aug 18, 2012 11:19:32 PM	No	0
☐	W3U2ZUQ	Aug 18, 2012 11:19:32 PM	No	0
☐	2K5IGV3	Aug 18, 2012 11:19:32 PM	No	0
☐	TOH3LL8	Aug 18, 2012 11:19:32 PM	No	0
☐	ASHB0CF	Aug 18, 2012 11:19:32 PM	No	0
☐	5AU9SC0	Aug 18, 2012 11:19:32 PM	No	0
☐	6SP4891	Aug 18, 2012 11:19:32 PM	No	0

Figure 3-13. Matching coupon codes listed in Magento

This example has shown how two powerful features of Magento—autogeneration of coupon codes and extending the REST-based API—can be leveraged to enhance the customer payment experience. The autogeneration of coupon codes provides a way of focusing marketing efforts. This added focus could provide rewards for customers in the payment process and encourage them to return to the online storefront.

See Also

Magento Shopping Cart Price Rules (*http://bit.ly/WmVZ5J*)

Magento "Introduction to Rest API" (*http://bit.ly/V3DIHo*)

Magento API – REST – OAuth Authentication (*http://bit.ly/T6hHv7*)

3.2. Making Payments with Preapprovals

Opportunity

For many types of businesses, a relationship is established between a buyer and seller in which the buyer may make multiple purchases over a period of time. Some of these models include software as a service and online game play, where new functionality or different levels of usage incur variable charges. Typically, either the customer will need to enter his payment information each time he makes a purchase, or the business will need to store payment information and regularly fulfill complicated PCI compliance requirements. Having to temporarily stop using a service to execute a payment can be disruptive and cause unnecessary work for the customer, and there is the potential for loss of revenue for the business if customers become frustrated and decide that the return is not worth the time and effort required.

Solution

One of the most powerful benefits of using a payment service such as PayPal is that PayPal handles the requirements of PCI compliance and is able to store payment information securely on behalf of businesses. Included in the PayPal offering is a preapproval payment flow by which a customer can allow a vendor to execute future payments on behalf of the customer. The payments can take place only in a particular time period and with limits in place. In this recipe we will look at how this preapproval payment flow works and a code example.

Discussion

The PayPal Adaptive Payments API provides an interface to the preapproval process, which can be leveraged for customer cases where multiple payments may happen over a period of time. The preapproval process, illustrated in Figure 3-14, consists of requesting a preapproval key from PayPal based on a set of payment parameters and then asking the customer to confirm the preapproval for payments by sending the customer to PayPal with the preapproval key. Once approved by the customer, the preapproval key can be used for future payments on that customer's behalf. Thus, the preapproval key should be stored with the customer record for use in future Pay API requests through the PayPal Adaptive Payments API.

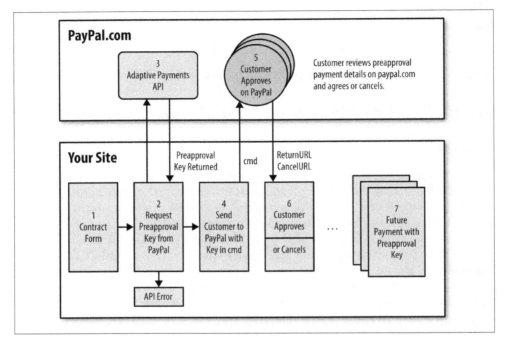

Figure 3-14. Preapproval payment flow

In this example, a form (*preapprovalForm.php*) will be used for demonstration purposes to set the required fields for the Adaptive Payments preapproval request. This would typically be handled by the business logic of your site behind the scenes. The form will then be posted to a handler page (*getPreapproval.php*), which will use the fields and the PayPal Adaptive Payments PHP SDK to request the preapproval key from PayPal. The minimum required fields for a preapproval request are:

startingDate

> The start date for this preapproval. The start date must be today or later, but not after the endingDate. The format is either Zulu time (UTC) or GMT.

endingDate

The ending date for this preapproval. The ending date must be later than the starting date but not more than a year from the starting date. The format is either Zulu time or GMT.

maxTotalAmountOfAllPayments

The maximum amount allowed for all payments under this preapproval.

currencyCode

The currency code for the payments.

returnUrl

The URL to return the user to on your site when the user has approved the preapproval on PayPal.

cancelUrl

The URL to return the user to on your site if the user cancels the approval process on PayPal.

requestEnvelope.errorLanguage

The language designation for any errors returned from the request. Must be en_US.

 The maximum total amount allowed for a preapproval is $2,000.00 in US dollars, or the equivalent in a different currency.

The entire list of fields, including optional fields, is available in PayPal's Preapproval API Operation (*http://bit.ly/SO6xxj*) documentation. One optional field is senderEmail, which is the email address of the PayPal user. This field is optional because the actual email address used to log into PayPal and pay may be different than that used with the website or application. However, this field can still be used, as the user can change the account information when she is forwarded to PayPal. Some other useful fields include the memo field for adding notes and the ipnNotificationUrl field, which will instruct the Preapproval API to send an Instant Payment Notification (IPN) to your backend systems (we'll see an example of this in Recipe 4.1, "Just-in-Time Shipping Forms").

Also available is a pinType field that informs PayPal that the customer must use a PIN code to allow each payment. Depending on the specific use case of your site, enabling this for customers may provide an added level of peace of mind. To enable PIN usage, the pinType field should be set to REQUIRED.

Example 3-7 shows the *preapprovalForm.php* page with the form, which asks for the optional senderEmail field and the required startingDate, endingDate, and maxTotalAmountOfAllPayments fields.

Example 3-7. preapprovalForm.php

```php
<?php
/************************************************************
preapprovalForm.php
Sample order form that kicks off a preapproval request.
Calls getPreapproval.php from form submittal.
************************************************************/
?>
<!DOCTYPE html>
<html>
<head>
<title>Preapproval Form</title>
<style>
* {margin: 0; padding: 0;}
body {background: #fff; color: #000;
  font: normal 62.5%/1.5 tahoma, verdana, sans-serif;}
h1 {font-size: 2.9em; font-weight: bold; margin: 1em 0 1em 10px;}
form {padding: 0 10px; width: 700px;}
legend {font-size: 2em; padding-left: 5px; padding-right: 5px;
  position: relative;}
fieldset {border: 1px solid #ccc; border-radius: 5px; float: left;
  padding: 10px; width: 320px;}
fieldset:nth-of-type(1) {margin-right: 10px;}
li {clear: both; list-style-type: none; margin: 0 0 10px;}
label, input {font-size: 1.3em;}
label {display: block; padding: 0 0 5px; width: 200px}
input { background-position: 295px 5px; background-repeat: no-repeat;
  border: 2px solid #ccc; border-radius: 5px;
  padding: 5px 25px 5px 5px; width: 285px;}
input:focus {outline: none;}
input:invalid:required { background-image: url(images/asterisk.png);
  box-shadow: none;}
input:focus:invalid {background-image: url(images/invalid.png);
  box-shadow: 0px 0px 5px #b01212; border: 2px solid #b01212;}
input:valid:required {background-image: url(images/accept.png);
  border: 2px solid #7ab526;}
input[type=number] {background-position: 275px 5px; text-align: left;}
div {clear: both; float: left; margin: 10px 0; text-align: center;
  width: 100%;}
div label {width: 100%;}
input[type=submit] {background: #7ab526; border: none;
  box-shadow: 0px 0px 5px #7ab526; color: #fff; cursor: pointer;
  font-size: 3em; font-weight: bold; margin: 20px auto; padding: 15px;
  width: auto;}
input[type=submit]:hover {box-shadow: 0px 0px 25px #7ab526;}
</style>
</head>
<body>
<h1>Enter the required preapproval information below.</h1>
  <form id="preapprovalForm" name="preapprovalForm"
    action="getPreapproval.php" method="post">
```

```
<fieldset>
  <legend>Preapproval Information</legend>
    <ol>
      <li>
        <label for="senderEmail">Sender's Email</label>
        <input type="text" size="50" maxlength="64" id="senderEmail"
          name="senderEmail" placeholder="Sandbox account email" />
      </li>
      <li>
        <label for="startingDate">Starting Date</label>
        <input type="date" required size="50" maxlength="32"
          id="startingDate" name="startingDate" value="" />
      </li>
      <li>
        <label for="endingDate">Ending Date</label>
        <input type="date" required size="50" maxlength="32"
          id="endingDate" name="endingDate" value="" />
      </li>
      <li>
        <label for="maxTotalAmountOfAllPayments">
        Maximum Total Amount
        </label>
        <input type="number" placeholder="&#36;" required min="0"
          max="2000" size="50" maxlength="32"
          id="maxTotalAmountOfAllPayments"
          name="maxTotalAmountOfAllPayments" value="" />
      </li>
    </ol>
    <div><input type="submit" value="Submit" /></div>
  </fieldset>
  </form>
</body>
</html>
```

When rendered in the browser, the form should appear as in Figure 3-15. Remember when testing the form that the starting date needs to be today or later, the ending date needs to be later than the start date but less than one year out, and the maximum total amount can not be above $2,000 USD. A constant value of en_US is used for the `curren cyCode` field in this example, but this could be dynamically set based on the region.

Example 3-8 shows the code for the preapproval processing page, *getPreapproval.php*. This page will perform the following tasks:

- Include the adaptive payments library and the *web_constants* library, which contains the constants for your application.
- Set the return and cancel URLs for the preapproval call.
- Package the request from the form fields and constants.

- Create an instance of the `AdaptivePayments` object and make the `Preapproval` method call.
- Check the call response for success and send the user to PayPal with the preapproval key in a `cmd` variable.

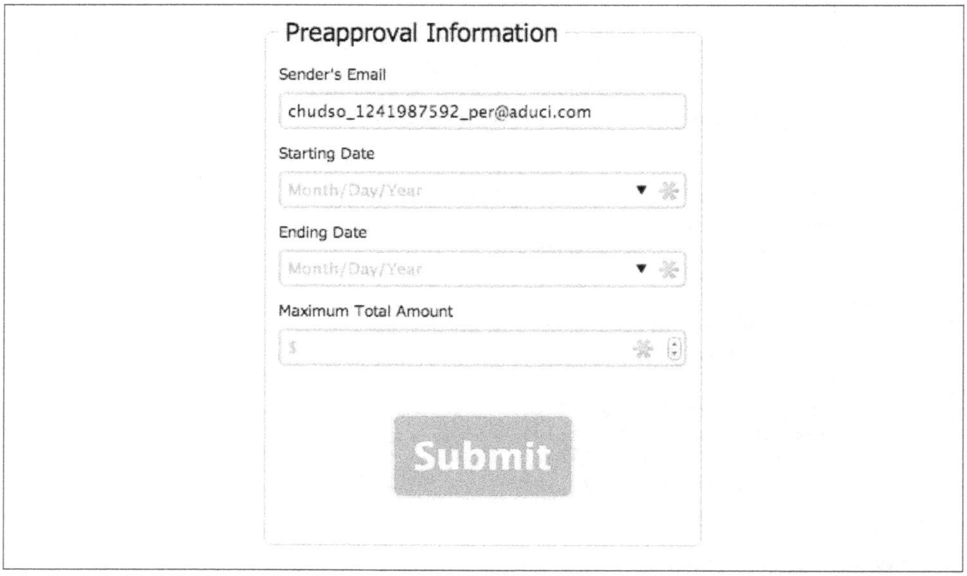

Figure 3-15. Preapproval form

Example 3-8. getPreapproval.php preapproval request page

```php
<?php

/***********************************************************
getPreapproval.php

This file creates the preapproval request, calls the PayPal
Adaptive Payments API for the preapproval key, and forwards
the user to paypal.com with the key upon success.

Called by preapprovalForm.php.

Calls APIError.php on error.
Forwards to paypal.com with cmd on success.
***********************************************************/

// Link to our AP library and constants files.
require_once 'lib/AdaptivePayments.php';
require_once 'web_constants.php';
```

```php
try {

  // Set our local server information for the return and cancel URLs.
  $serverName = $_SERVER['SERVER_NAME'];
  $serverPort = $_SERVER['SERVER_PORT'];
  $url=dirname(
    'http://'.$serverName.':'.$serverPort.$_SERVER['REQUEST_URI']);

  // Set the return and cancel URLs for the user returning from PayPal.
  $returnURL = $url."/yourReturn.php";
  $cancelURL = $url."/preapprovalForm.php";

  // Create a new preapproval request and fill in entries.
  $preapprovalRequest = new preapprovalRequest();

  // Determine if senderEmail is provided.
  if ($_POST['senderEmail'] != "") {
    $preapprovalRequest->senderEmail = $_POST['senderEmail'];
  }
  $preapprovalRequest->startingDate = $_POST['startingDate']."Z";
  $preapprovalRequest->endingDate = $_POST['endingDate']."Z";
  $preapprovalRequest->maxTotalAmountOfAllPayments =
    $_POST['maxTotalAmountOfAllPayments'];
  $preapprovalRequest->currencyCode = "USD";
  $preapprovalRequest->memo = "Preapproval example.";

  // Set the cancel and return URLs.
  $preapprovalRequest->cancelUrl = $cancelURL ;
  $preapprovalRequest->returnUrl = $returnURL;

  // Add the required request envelope error language setting.
  $preapprovalRequest->requestEnvelope = new RequestEnvelope();
  $preapprovalRequest->requestEnvelope->errorLanguage = "en_US";

  // Create the adaptive payments object and call Preapproval.
  $ap = new AdaptivePayments();
  $response=$ap->Preapproval($preapprovalRequest);

  // Check for success of Preapproval call.
  if (strtoupper($ap->isSuccess) == 'SUCCESS') {
    // Call was successful, retrieve preapproval key and forward
    // user to PayPal.
    $PAKey = $response->preapprovalKey;
    $payPalURL =
      PAYPAL_REDIRECT_URL.'_ap-preapproval&preapprovalkey='.$PAKey;
    header("Location: ".$payPalURL);
  } else {
    // Call failed, show APIError message.
    $_SESSION['FAULTMSG']=$ap->getLastError();
    $location = "APIError.php";
    header("Location: $location");
```

```
    }
}
catch(Exception $ex) {
  // Catch any operation exceptions and show error.
  $fault = new FaultMessage();
  $errorData = new ErrorData();
  $errorData->errorId = $ex->getFile() ;
  $errorData->message = $ex->getMessage();
  $fault->error = $errorData;
  $_SESSION['FAULTMSG']=$fault;
  $location = "APIError.php";
  header("Location: $location");
}
?>
```

When the preapproval request is performed, a `PreapprovalResponse` object is returned. The response object contains a `responseEnvelope` with an `ack` for success or failure. If the call was successful, the `PreapprovalResponse` object will contain a `preapproval Key` property containing a string value starting with `PA` (for Preapproval), as seen in Example 3-9.

Example 3-9. PreapprovalResponse object

```
PreapprovalResponse Object (
  [responseEnvelope] => ResponseEnvelope Object (
    [timestamp] => 2012-08-16T07:43:31.599-07:00
    [ack] => Success
    [correlationId] => f55c60f33156d
    [build] => 3392538
  )
  [preapprovalKey] => PA-41F84046H74869237
)
```

 Upon receiving a preapproval key back from the Adaptive Payments API, you should store it in your database record associated with the customer so that it can be used later for payment purposes. If the user cancels out of the authorization process, however, the preapproval key should be removed since the user has decided to cancel the agreement. It is also a good idea to keep the start and end dates in the database with the key, along with any other parameters for the preapproval, for use in the payment logic of your application and maintenance of the customer record.

Requesting and receiving the preapproval key is only the first part of setting up the preapproval payments agreement; the user will still need to accept the agreement in his PayPal account. To accomplish this, the *getPreapproval.php* page forwards to the user to the PayPal site (in this case, the sandbox site for testing purposes) with a query string including the *cmd=_ap-preapproval* and *preapprovalkey=PA-...* fields:

> *https://www.sandbox.paypal.com/webscr&cmd=_ap-preapproval&preapprovalkey=PA-41F84046H74869237*

The *cmd* key informs PayPal that a preapproval validation is taking place via the Adaptive Payments API (*_ap*) for the preapproval key provided. When forwarded to PayPal, the user is asked to log in. Once logged in, the user is shown a summary of the preapproval payment and asked to Approve or Cancel, as seen in Figure 3-16.

Figure 3-16. Preapproval payment agreement acceptance

If the customer accepts the agreement, he will be forwarded to the `returnUrl` that was provided in the original preapproval request. If instead the customer cancels the preapproval, he will be forwarded to the `cancelUrl` address that was provided with the preapproval request.

Once a preapproval has been set, the details of the preapproval can be retrieved via the PreapprovalDetails API Operation (*http://bit.ly/ UAuunJ*), using the `preapprovalKey` that was acquired on the original preapproval request.

To validate that the preapproval payment agreement has been set correctly, log into your sandbox test site as the payee user. Once logged into the sandbox interface, go to Profile → My Preapproved Payments → Preapproved Payment Plans. Displayed in the "My Preapproved Payments" section should be the agreement that was just created, as seen in Figure 3-17.

Figure 3-17. New preapproval payment agreement

If you select the agreement in the list of preapproved payments, the details will be shown for that agreement, including the start and end dates (see Figure 3-18).

Figure 3-18. Preapproved payment details

Now that the preapproval payments agreement is in place, future `Pay` requests can be performed through the PayPal API with the preapproval key on behalf of the customer. This will provide for a smooth and simple payment process for the customer inside the website or application.

> Since a customer can cancel a preapproval payments agreement through the PayPal account interface at any time, it is a good practice to use the PayPal Instant Payment Notification capability when creating a preapproval to ensure that any changes to the preapproval payments will be sent to the backend of your site so you can update your customers' accounts. See Recipe 4.1, "Just-in-Time Shipping Forms" for a sample of receiving IPNs from PayPal and processing the data.

See Also

PayPal Integration Center "Preapproval API Operation" (*https://cms.paypal.com/us/cgi-bin/?cmd=_render-content&content_ID=developer/e_howto_api_APPreapproval*)

PayPal Adaptive Payments Developer Guide (*https://cms.paypal.com/cms_content/US/en_US/files/developer/PP_AdaptivePayments.pdf*)

PayPal Developer Network "Preapproval API Operation" (*https://www.x.com/developers/paypal/documentation-tools/api/preapproval-api-operation*)

PayPal Integration Center "PreapprovalDetails API Operation" (*http://bit.ly/UAuunJ*)

PayPal Instant Payment Notification (*https://www.paypal.com/ipn*)

3.3. Giving Back at Checkout

Opportunity

In checkout lines at many brick-and-mortar stores we are presented with opportunities to donate to local and global charities, contributing to the social good when we make a purchase. This trend has spilled over to online sales, and merchants are finding that being connected with a social cause can create an increased positive experience for customers when they check out. Providing an option to contribute in the online checkout flow can be a powerful method of creating a strong bond with customers.

Solution

The PayPal Adaptive Payments API provides a method for a single user to make payments to multiple recipients in one transaction call. This form of transaction is aptly named *parallel* or *split payments* and would typically be used when a vendor aggregates products or services from multiple vendors that are displayed directly to the user. A common example is a travel agent who may create a package of airline tickets and hotel and car rentals. Even though there is one price for the package, that amount is split between multiple vendors, with different amounts paid in parallel to each. In the consumer's account, there will be a distinct payment per supplier of each particular service. In this example we will use parallel payments to allow the customer to pay the vendor and a selected charity in a single API call.

Discussion

The scenario is as follows. A customer is ready to check out on a site after selecting multiple products. During the checkout process, the customer is presented with a form similar to the one in Figure 3-19. The customer can check the box signifying that she would like to contribute to a cause and then select a specific cause and dollar amount to contribute. Upon paying for the order, the donation is added to the total purchase price. However, the user will get two receipts via email: one from the vendor from which the products were purchased and one from the charity to which the donation was given. On the customer's transaction record, two separate transactions will have occurred, even though the customer input her payment details only once. More importantly, the donation portion will go straight from the customer to the charity (rather than through the vendor), making the process simple for all parties.

Figure 3-19. Donation form on checkout

In this example we will create the form, which will then be posted and perform the parallel payment with PayPal. Example 3-10 shows the code for the donation form to be displayed on checkout.

Example 3-10. donateOption.php donate on checkout form

```php
<?php
/***********************************************************
donateOption.php

Sample form for donation option on checkout.

Calls doParallelPmt.php from form submittal.

***********************************************************/
?>

<!DOCTYPE html>
<html>
<head>
<title>Donate on Checkout Form</title>
<style>
```

```
* {margin: 0; padding: 0;}
body {background: #fff; color: #000;
  font: normal 62.5%/1.5 tahoma, verdana, sans-serif;}
h1 {font-size: 2.9em; font-weight: bold; margin: 1em 0 1em 10px;}
form {padding: 0 10px; width: 700px;}
legend {font-size: 2em; padding-left: 5px; padding-right: 5px;
  position: relative;}
fieldset {border: 1px solid #ccc; border-radius: 5px; float: left;
  padding: 10px; width: 320px;}
fieldset:nth-of-type(1) {margin-right: 10px;}
li {clear: both; list-style-type: none; margin: 0 0 10px;}
label, input {font-size: 1.3em;}
label {display: block; padding: 0 0 5px; width: 200px}
input {background-position: 295px 5px; background-repeat: no-repeat;
  border: 2px solid #ccc; border-radius: 5px;
  padding: 5px 25px 5px 5px; width: 285px;}
input:focus {outline: none;}
input:invalid:required {background-image: url(images/asterisk.png);
  box-shadow: none;}
input:focus:invalid {background-image: url(images/invalid.png);
  box-shadow: 0px 0px 5px #b01212; border: 2px solid #b01212;}
input:valid:required {background-image: url(images/accept.png);
  border: 2px solid #7ab526;}
input[type=number] {background-position: 275px 5px; text-align: left;}
input[type=checkbox] {font-size: 2em; text-align: left; width: 20px;}
div {clear: both; float: left; margin: 10px 0; text-align: center;
  width: 100%;}
div label {width: 100%;}
input[type=submit] {background: #7ab526; border: none;
  box-shadow: 0px 0px 5px #7ab526; color: #fff; cursor: pointer;
  font-size: 3em; font-weight: bold; margin: 20px auto; padding: 15px;
  width: auto;}
input[type=submit]:hover {box-shadow: 0px 0px 25px #7ab526;}
</style>
</head>
<body>
  <form id="donationForm" name="donationForm"
    action="doParallelPmt.php" method="post">
  <fieldset>
    <legend>Contribute to a Cause?</legend>
    <ol>
      <li>
        <input type="checkbox" id="flagDonation" name="flagDonation"
          value="1" />
        Yes I would like to contribute.
      </li>
      <li>
        <label for="charityEmail">Select a charity:</label>
        <select id="charityEmail" name="charityEmail">
          <option value="donate@childsplaycharity.org">
            Child's Play (childsplaycharity.org)
            </option>
```

```
          <option value="servic_1241987644_biz@aduci.com">
            My Charity (mycharity.org)
          </option>
        </select>
      </li>
      <li>
        <label for="donation">Donation Amount</label>
        <input type="number" placeholder="&#36;" min="1" max="1000"
          size="50" id="donation" name="donation" value="1" />
      </li>
    </ol>
    <div><input type="submit" value="Submit" /></div>
  </fieldset>
  </form>
</body>
</html>
```

To create a parallel payment, the code will need to know the recipient's registered PayPal email address. Thus, in the donation form, when the user selects the charity the value set is actually the charity's PayPal email address. For this example the select box has one real option, which is the Child's Play charity, and one testing email address, which coincides with a testing account that has been set up in the PayPal sandbox. (To learn about setting up test accounts in the PayPal sandbox, see the online PayPal Sandbox Documentation (*http://bit.ly/UPl7Ru*).)

Once the customer has selected the charity, added the amount of the donation, and clicked "Submit," the form will be posted to a processing page. The processing page will use the PayPal Adaptive Payments PHP SDK library to facilitate a simple call to the Pay API method with the parallel payments information. In the processing page the code will perform the following steps:

1. Create the cancel and return URLs for the call to the PayPal Adaptive Payments API.

2. Create a new PayRequest instance and set the sender email, return and cancel URLs, currency code, and client details.

3. Set the payment receivers in a receiver array.

4. Add the receiver array to the PayRequest.

5. Set the fee allocation model and memo.

6. Make the call to the Adaptive Payments API.

Example 3-11 shows the code for the processing page, *doParallelPmt.php*.

Example 3-11. doParallelPmt.php parallel payment call

```
<?php
/**************************************************
```

```
doParallelPmt.php

Called by donateOption.php.
Calls  APIError.php on error.

Based on PayParallelReceipt.php from SDK Samples.
*************************************************/

require_once 'lib/AdaptivePayments.php';
require_once 'web_constants.php';

session_start();

try {

    /* Set our store PayPal ID (seller email) for receiving the order
       payment. Also set the total sale amount for the order and the
       buyer's email. These would normally come from a customer database
       and the shopping cart.*/
    $recEmailSeller = 'wppm_13411073_biz@aduci.com';
    $totalSale = 218.73;
    $senderEmail = "chudso_12419875_per@aduci.com";

    /* Set the return and cancel URLs, instructing PayPal where to
       return the user upon payment confirmation or cancellation.*/
    $serverName = $_SERVER['SERVER_NAME'];
    $serverPort = $_SERVER['SERVER_PORT'];
    $url=dirname(
      'http://'.$serverName.':'.$serverPort.$_SERVER['REQUEST_URI']);
    $returnURL = $url."/PaymentDetails.php";
    $cancelURL = $url."/donateOption.php" ;

    /* Create the actual pay request with our URLs, client details,
       currency code, buyer's email, and request envelope.*/
    $payRequest = new PayRequest();
    $payRequest->actionType = "PAY";
    $payRequest->cancelUrl = $cancelURL ;
    $payRequest->returnUrl = $returnURL;
    $payRequest->clientDetails = new ClientDetailsType();
    $payRequest->clientDetails->applicationId = APPLICATION_ID;
    $payRequest->clientDetails->deviceId = DEVICE_ID;
    $payRequest->clientDetails->ipAddress = "127.0.0.1";
    $payRequest->currencyCode = "USD";
    $payRequest->senderEmail = $senderEmail;
    $payRequest->requestEnvelope = new RequestEnvelope();
    $payRequest->requestEnvelope->errorLanguage = "en_US";

    // Create our receiver list for parallel payments.
    $receiverList = array();

    /* Set the store as the first receiver with the shopping
       cart total sale. The order of receivers does not matter but
```

```php
   having the main store first keeps it logical.*/
$receiver0 = new receiver();
$receiver0->email = $recEmailSeller;
$receiver0->amount = $totalSale;
$receiverList[0] = $receiver0;

// Check if a charity donation has been selected.
if ($_POST['flagDonation'] == 1) {
  // If so, then create a secondary receiver for the donation.
  $receiver1 = new receiver();
  $receiver1->email = $_POST['charityEmail'];
  $receiver1->amount = $_POST['donation'];
  $receiverList[1] = $receiver1;
}

// Add the receiver list into the pay request.
$payRequest->receiverList = $receiverList;

/* Set optional Pay Request fields. The feesPayer with
   EACHRECEIVER instructs PayPal that each receiver will cover
   their fees for the portion of the payment. Non-profits for
   the donation have discounted fees with PayPal.*/
$payRequest->feesPayer = "EACHRECEIVER";
$payRequest->memo = "Donation via yoursite.com.";

/* Make the call to PayPal to get the Pay token.
   If the API call succeeded, then redirect the buyer to PayPal
   to begin to authorize payment. If an error occured, show the
   resulting errors.*/
$ap = new AdaptivePayments();
$response=$ap->Pay($payRequest);

// Check the return of the request and handle appropriately.
if (strtoupper($ap->isSuccess) == 'FAILURE') {
  $_SESSION['FAULTMSG']=$ap->getLastError();
  $location = "APIError.php";
  header("Location: $location");
} else {
  $_SESSION['payKey'] = $response->payKey;
  if ($response->paymentExecStatus == "COMPLETED") {
    $location = "PaymentDetails.php";
    header("Location: $location");
  } else {
    $token = $response->payKey;

    // Important to pass _ap-payment command and paykey to PayPal.
    $payPalURL = PAYPAL_REDIRECT_URL.'_ap-payment&paykey='.$token;
    header("Location: ".$payPalURL);
  }
}
}
}
catch(Exception $ex) {
```

```
    $fault = new FaultMessage();
    $errorData = new ErrorData();
    $errorData->errorId = $ex->getFile() ;
    $errorData->message = $ex->getMessage();
    $fault->error = $errorData;
    $_SESSION['FAULTMSG']=$fault;
    $location = "APIError.php";
    header("Location: $location");
}
?>
```

For testing purposes, after the `try` statement the code sets the vendor's email as the `recEmailSeller` variable, the total sale of the cart (as `totalSale`), and the customer's PayPal email address (`senderEmail`). In a real scenario these would be set from your shopping cart and customer database.

In the processing page, there is one key difference that makes this a parallel payment: when creating the `PayRequest`, the recipients of the payments are listed in the receiver array with their corresponding PayPal email addresses and the amount that goes to each recipient. In this example the code is informing the PayPal API that the sender is requesting funds to be sent to each recipient, in the amount listed for each in the call. Normal transaction fees apply, but the fees can be assigned in multiple ways. In this case we want each recipient to handle its proportion of the fees, so we will designate the EACHRECEIVER flag. The possible fee models are:

EACHRECEIVER
    Each receiver pays its proportion of the fees (default).

PRIMARYRECEIVER
    The primary receiver of the funds pays all fees.

SECONDARYONLY
    The secondary receivers pay all fees, proportionally.

SENDER
    The sender pays all fees.

For a complete guide to the different fee model options, see the PayPal Adaptive Payments Developer Guide (*https://cms.paypal.com/cms_content/US/en_US/files/develop er/PP_AdaptivePayments.pdf*). The additional benefit in this case is that a registered charity receives discounts on the normal transaction fees, so the fee for the amount donated to the charity will be discounted.

The PayPal Adaptive Payments API provides for both parallel and chained payments. The main technical difference between the two is that for chained payments a relationship between payment recipients is created via a `primary` receiver property, which can be set to `true` or `false`. Chained payments are discussed and illustrated in Recipe 4.3, "Multiple Supplier Fulfillment".

The processing page also incorporates a *web_constants.php* file, which has the PayPal sandbox URL and credentials that will get swapped or dynamically replaced with the production credentials when ready.

 To use the Adaptive Payments API in production, your application will need approval from PayPal.

To test the parallel payments process, load the form page in your browser and select to contribute, then select the charity and enter a donation amount. When you submit the form, the processing page will package the request and perform the `Pay` call to the PayPal Adaptive Payments API. Upon successful completion, the processing page will then send you (the customer) to PayPal with a `cmd` option of `_ap-payment`, instructing PayPal that you need to approve a payment request made through the Adaptive Payments API. To uniquely identify this request, the pay key returned from the `Pay` request is also appended. When a user is directed to PayPal with this information, a screen similar to Figure 3-20 asking the user to log into his PayPal account is displayed.

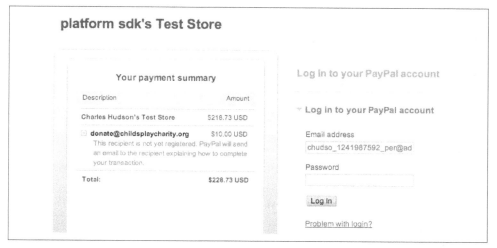

Figure 3-20. User asked to log in on parallel payment

Notice that the individual payments and the total amount are noted in the PayPal landing page. In this case, since we are using the sandbox, *donate@childsplaycharity.org* is not recognized as a testing account. In a production environment, this would not be the case.

After logging in, the customer will be asked to Pay or Cancel the payment, as shown in Figure 3-21.

Figure 3-21. Payment summary

If the user cancels the payment verification process, he will be returned to the URL designated in the `cancelUrl` variable of the initial `Pay` request. If the user successfully makes the payment, he will be returned to the URL designated in the `returnUrl` field.

To validate that the payments were performed separately, log in as the test user who made the payments and check the history in the account in the sandbox. You will see one payment to the vendor account and a separate payment to the charity account. Using parallel payments to add a donation form to the checkout process is really this easy, and it can improve the overall experience for the buyer while raising some funds for good causes.

See Also

PayPal Adaptive Payments Developer Guide (*https://cms.paypal.com/cms_content/US/ en_US/files/developer/PP_AdaptivePayments.pdf*)

PayPal Integration Center "Pay API Operation" (*https://cms.paypal.com/us/cgi-bin/? cmd=_render-content&content_ID=developer/e_howto_api_APPayAPI*)

PayPal Adaptive Payments PHP SDK (*https://www.x.com/developers/paypal/ documentation-tools/paypal-sdk-index#adaptivepaymentsnew*)

3.4. Conclusion

The purchase stage is the step in the commerce lifecycle when a potential customer enters into a paid relationship with the vendor. This step can be both an emotional and a physical hurdle, based on the complexities of the purchase process. However, through the use of various APIs the process can be shortened and, as we have seen from the examples in this chapter, cemented quickly with an overall positive experience. New customers entering into a relationship with the vendor will expect the overall value of completing the purchase to be greater than the time and effort expended. Customers should not have to think twice about whether putting in the time and effort required to complete the purchase process is worth it, but instead should be brought quickly to the next stage, having their orders fulfilled.

CHAPTER 4

Order Fulfillment

The fourth stage in the simplified commerce lifecycle, as shown in Figure 4-1, involves the fulfillment, shipment, and receipt of orders. Merchants sometimes consider the steps after the purchase transaction as simply routine actions to fulfill the order, and think that at this point the work of receiving a new order and cementing a new customer relationship is complete. However, given the competitive landscape of the Internet and the ease with which consumers can review their experiences with a merchant, this step in the commerce lifecycle is critical to establishing an extensive base of repeat customers and referrals.

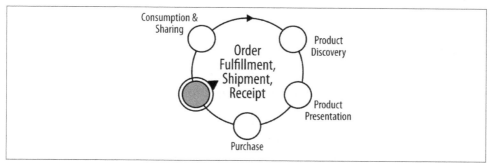

Figure 4-1. Simplified commerce lifecycle—stage 4

The range of APIs available to support the fulfillment process is growing rapidly as third-party payment providers, shipping firms, and merchants recognize the value of providing tighter integration into their platforms through APIs. In this chapter we will look at streamlining the fulfillment process through automated notifications for faster packaging, adding flexible shipping options to a Magento cart, and delivering orders faster by leveraging chained payments through PayPal to pay suppliers. In the end, this automation and the added efficiency due to the use of APIs can result in a simpler process for the merchant, and a positive customer experience.

4.1. Just-in-Time Shipping Forms

Opportunity

In the back office, several processes are triggered once the sale of a product takes place. Automating these tasks can reduce the time taken and any errors in fulfilling orders. It would be helpful if there were a way to determine automatically when a transaction cleared, was rejected, or was cancelled so that shipping slips could be printed, emails automatically sent, and accounts updated.

Solution

As part of a PayPal business account, merchants have access to a service for automated notifications: the Instant Payment Notification, or IPN for short. This service is able to notify a URL on the merchant's side of transaction status changes and pass along specific order information. In this example we will use the IPN service to notify a web page when transactions are completed. If the transaction is via a shopping cart and has a completed status, the page will create a shipping slip or invoice based on a previously designed template. The shipping invoices can then be emailed, printed, or reviewed in an administration interface.

Discussion

When a transaction is performed on behalf of a business by PayPal, whether through a virtual terminal, express checkout, recurring payment, or some other form, a notification can be sent from the PayPal servers to a handler or listener web page. The notification is built as a posted series of key and value pairs. The fields contain a variety of information including the transaction ID, type, and payment status. Depending on the transaction type and status, the data transmitted can include shipping information, detailed shopping cart information (item name, quantity), and currency information.

After receiving an IPN, your listener will need to post the IPN back to PayPal in a validation request. There are two reasons for posting the IPN back to PayPal:

1. Validation of the authenticity of the IPN
2. Verification for PayPal that the IPN was received

If your listener does not ask PayPal to verify the IPN, there is the potential that a fictitious IPN could be injected into your listener, which could kick off any automated processing in place. When the PayPal servers receive the validation request, they will mark the request as either valid or invalid based on what was sent in the IPN. If the IPN is verified, you can parse out the values, store the information in database tables for orders, message other back office systems, and kick off other processes (such as creating a shipping form, as demonstrated in this solution). This IPN flow is illustrated in Figure 4-2.

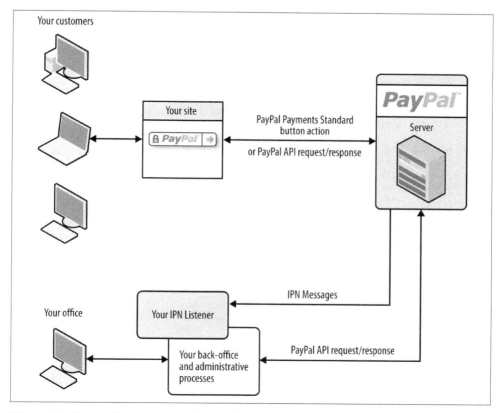

Figure 4-2. Instant Payment Notification flow

In this example, a PHP file will be installed on the web server to handle notifications from PayPal. When a notification is sent to the listener, the IPN data will be processed and a static shipping invoice HTML page will be created in a *slips* directory. The structure of the invoice is based on *shipping_slip.html*, which is a template shipping invoice HTML file.

To create your IPN listener, open an empty PHP file named *IPNListener.php*. This will be the page in the URL that you direct PayPal to send the IPNs to when notifications occur. Add the code in Example 4-1 to the file.

Example 4-1. IPNListener.php

```php
<?php
/***************************************************
IPNListener.php

This file receives IPNs from PayPal and processes
them. Since this is from server to server, there is
no UI for this file. The only output is the log file,
which is for basic logging only.

***************************************************/

// flag to define if working in sandbox (debug mode)
$FLG_DEBUG_MODE = true;

// set our log file (could replace with PEAR)
$logfile = "./IPNListener.log";
$fh = fopen($logfile, 'a') or die("can't open log file");

logWrite("New IPN");

// create validate request with command
$req = 'cmd=' . urlencode('_notify-validate');

// add back all fields of the posted string
foreach ($_POST as $key => $value) {
  $value = urlencode(stripslashes($value));
  $req .= "&$key=$value";
}

// set if using the sandbox or production for validation
if ($FLG_DEBUG_MODE) {
  $val_server = 'https://www.sandbox.paypal.com/cgi-bin/webscr';
} else {
  $val_server = 'https://www.paypal.com/cgi-bin/webscr';
}

// launch the curl request to PayPal servers to verify
$ch = curl_init();
curl_setopt($ch, CURLOPT_URL, $val_server);
curl_setopt($ch, CURLOPT_HEADER, 0);
curl_setopt($ch, CURLOPT_POST, 1);
curl_setopt($ch, CURLOPT_RETURNTRANSFER,1);
curl_setopt($ch, CURLOPT_POSTFIELDS, $req);
curl_setopt($ch, CURLOPT_SSL_VERIFYPEER, 1);
curl_setopt($ch, CURLOPT_SSL_VERIFYHOST, 2);
$res = curl_exec($ch);
```

```
curl_close($ch);

// check if PayPal verified the IPN received
if (strcmp ($res, "VERIFIED") == 0) {

  // log out IPN in a JSON format
  logWrite("Verified: " . json_encode($_POST));

  // assign posted variables to local variables
  $txn_id         = $_POST['txn_id'];
  $txn_type       = $_POST['txn_type'];
  $payment_status = $_POST['payment_status'];
  $receiver_email = $_POST['receiver_email'];

  // TODO: check that receiver_email is your primary PayPal email

  // dispatch based on status of payment
  switch ($payment_status) {

    case "Completed":
      // completed sale

      // TODO: check that payment_amount/payment_currency are correct
      // TODO: check that txn_id has not been previously processed

      // check if the type of transaction is cart
      if ($txn_type == 'cart') {

        // set up our holding arrays for keys and values
        $arrShipKeys   = array();
        $arrShipValues = array();

        // set our shipping header information
        array_push($arrShipKeys, "<<DATE>>");
        array_push($arrShipValues, date("M j, Y",
          strtotime($_POST['payment_date'])));

        array_push($arrShipKeys, "<<STATUS>>");
        array_push($arrShipValues, "PAID");

        array_push($arrShipKeys, "<<TXNID>>");
        array_push($arrShipValues, $txn_id);

        // get payer information and add to arrays
        // TODO: check if following funcs required
        $first_name     = $_POST['first_name'];
        $last_name      = $_POST['last_name'];
        $payer_email    = $_POST['payer_email'];
        $address_street = $_POST['address_street'];
        $address_city   = $_POST['address_city'];
        $address_state  = $_POST['address_state'];
        $address_zip    = $_POST['address_zip'];
```

```php
$address_country = $_POST['address_country'];

array_push($arrShipKeys, "<<ADDRESS>>");
array_push($arrShipValues, $first_name . " " . $last_name .
  "<br/>" . $address_street . "<br/>" . $address_city . ", " .
  $address_state . " " . $address_zip . "<br/>" .
  $address_country);

// get rest of transaction details
$shipping_method = $_POST['shipping_method'];
if (isset($_POST['num_cart_items'])) {
  $num_cart_items = $_POST['num_cart_items'];
} elseif ($FLG_DEBUG_MODE) {
  // catch defect with simulator-based IPN
  $num_cart_items = 1;
} else {
  $num_cart_items = 0;
}

// get the items in the cart
$subtotal = 0;
$items = "";

for ($i=1; $i<=$num_cart_items; $i+=1) {

  // get fields of items in transaction and store each set
  $item_order_id = $i;
  $item_number   = $_POST['item_number'.$i];
  $item_name     = $_POST['item_name'.$i];
  $quantity      = $_POST['quantity'.$i];
  $mc_gross      = $_POST['mc_gross_'.$i];

  $subtotal += $mc_gross;

  $items .= '<tr><td align="right" valign="top"
    class="borderBottomLeftRight"><p class="sliptabledata">' .
    $item_number . '</p></td>' . '<td align="left" valign="top"
    class="borderBottomRight"><p class="sliptabledata">' .
    $item_name . '</p></td>' . '<td align="center" valign="top"
    class="borderBottomRight"><p class="sliptabledata">' .
    $quantity . '</p></td>' . '<td align="right" valign="top"
    class="borderBottomRight"><p class="sliptabledata">' .
    $mc_gross . '</p></td>' . '</tr>';
}
array_push($arrShipKeys, "<<ITEMS>>");
array_push($arrShipValues, $items);

// set the financial section numbers
array_push($arrShipKeys, "<<SUBTOTAL>>");
array_push($arrShipValues, number_format($subtotal,2));

$mc_shipping = $_POST['mc_shipping'];
```

```
      if ($mc_shipping == "") {
        $mc_shipping = 0;
      }
      array_push($arrShipKeys, "<<SHIPPING>>");
      array_push($arrShipValues, number_format($mc_shipping,2));

      $mc_handling = $_POST['mc_handling'];
      if ($mc_handling == "") {
        $mc_handling = 0;
      }
      array_push($arrShipKeys, "<<HANDLING>>");
      array_push($arrShipValues, number_format($mc_handling,2));

      $tax = $_POST['tax'];
      if ($tax == "") {
        $tax = 0;
      }
      array_push($arrShipKeys, "<<TAX>>");
      array_push($arrShipValues, number_format($tax,2));

      $mc_gross = $_POST['mc_gross'];
      array_push($arrShipKeys, "<<TOTAL>>");
      array_push($arrShipValues, $mc_gross);

      // finished parsing IPN
      logWrite("Finished IPN");

      // call the function to create shipping label
      createShipping($txn_id, $arrShipKeys, $arrShipValues);

    }  // end if txn_type is cart

  break;

  // some other possible IPN transaction statuses:
  case "Reversed":
    // sale was reversed - mark order as such
  break;

  case "Refunded":
    // refunded: you refunded the payment
  break;

  }  // end switch payment status

} else if (strcmp ($res, "INVALID") == 0) {

  // PayPal responded with invalid request
  logWrite("INVALID REQUEST: " . json_encode($_POST));
}

// close log file
```

```
  fclose($fh);

// function to create the shipping form
function createShipping($txn_id, $arrShipKeys, $arrShipValues) {

  // read in template file
  $ship_contents = file_get_contents("shipping_slip.html");

  // verify the template was read in
  if($ship_contents) {

    // merge in fields from IPN
    $ship_contents = str_replace($arrShipKeys, $arrShipValues,
      $ship_contents);

    // set output file to txn # and output merged content
    $shipping_file = "./slips/" . $txn_id . ".html";
    file_put_contents($shipping_file, $ship_contents);
  }
}

// function to add log entry
function logWrite($log_msg) {
  global $fh;
  $log_entry = date("y/m/d G:i:s") . " - " . $log_msg . "\n";
  fwrite($fh, $log_entry);
}
?>
```

To prevent security issues and the possible injection of fictitious IPNs, the first action taken when the file receives an IPN is to repackage the posted fields of the transaction from PayPal and ask the PayPal servers to verify that the IPN is valid. If a validation request is not sent back to the PayPal system, PayPal will attempt to resend the IPN for a period of time.

To request PayPal validation of the IPN, cURL is used to send the IPN fields in a new query string containing an additional key and value, *cmd=_notify-validate*. The addition of this new key and value asks the PayPal servers to validate the IPN that was received as having come from PayPal:

```
<?php
// create validate request with command
$req = 'cmd=' . urlencode('_notify-validate');

// add back all fields of the posted string
foreach ($_POST as $key => $value) {
  $value = urlencode(stripslashes($value));
  $req .= "&$key=$value";
}
```

In this example a log file is used for debugging purposes since the IPN listener being called by PayPal will not display any visual queue when an IPN is received. In the log file we will put brief messages, including a JSON version of the IPN payload. To read the payload of a received IPN copy, paste the JSON into a JSON viewer (*http://www.jsonview er.com*).

You can replace this logger with a more powerful and production-ready version using PEAR or the like.

In this code a flag is added, `$FLAG_DEBUG_MODE`, to indicate whether we are running in debug mode. PayPal provides a testing sandbox here (*https://developer.paypal.com*) from which we can send test IPNs, as we will explore later. The script sets the correct endpoint based on the mode in which we are running. This allows you to test your IPN handler by sending and validating IPNs from the PayPal sandbox prior to releasing the handler to production, at which time you would set the debug flag to `false`.

It is a good practice to give the listener file an obscure name and to have the file located in an orphaned, unsearchable directory so that anyone looking will not accidentally locate it.

Upon receiving a response from PayPal and validating that the IPN is `VERIFIED`, the script will log the JSON version of the payload and begin to parse the payload fields. Before getting too far into the transaction, however, the script checks the `payment_status` to determine if this is a `Completed` transaction, meaning that a payment has been successful. PayPal provides IPNs on several different transaction statuses and types. You can review the list of available payment statuses and transaction types in the online documentation (*http://bit.ly/V3IqoA*). In this case we want to also check that this is a completed payment from a shopping cart, so the code also verifies that the transaction type is of type `cart` (`$txn_type=='cart'`).

Once all the fields have been parsed and pushed into arrays with their corresponding keys for the shipping form template, the script calls the `createShipping` function, passing in the transaction ID and arrays. The `createShipping` function then reads in the template HTML file, *shipping_slip.html* (Example 4-2), and replaces the matching keys from the key array with the corresponding values in the value array. The newly merged shipping invoice is then saved out to a new file in the *slips* directory and named with the unique transaction ID provided by PayPal.

Example 4-2. Shipping invoice template

```
<!DOCTYPE html>
<html>
```

```html
<head>
<meta charset="UTF-8" />
<title>Shipping Invoice Template</title>
<style>
body {font-family: Verdana, Arial, Helvetica, sans-serif;
  font-size: 10pt; margin:50px 0px; padding:0px; text-align:center;}
H1 {margin: 0px; font-weight: bold; font-size: 18px; color: #332B26;}
label {display: block; padding: 0 0 5px; width: 110px;}
#slip {width: 744px; margin: 0px auto; text-align: left;
  padding: 15px;}
.sliptableheader {margin: 5px 10px 5px 10px; font-weight: bold;}
.sliptabledata {margin: 5px 10px 5px 10px;}
#shipto {clear: both; padding-top: 40px}
#shipto legend {font-size: 1.1em; padding-left: 5px;
  padding-right: 5px; position: relative;}
#shipto fieldset {border: 1px solid #000; border-radius: 5px;
  float: left; padding: 10px; width: 360px;}
#invoice {float:right}
#invoice legend {font-size: 1.5em; position: relative;
  text-align:right}
#invoice fieldset {border: 1px solid #000; border-radius: 5px;
  width: 250px; padding: 10px}
#invoice li {clear: both; list-style-type: none; margin: 0;
  padding: 0;}
#invoice ol {padding: 0; margin:0}
#invoice label {display: block; padding: 5px; width: 63px;
  border: 1px solid #000; float:left; text-align:right}
#invoice span {display: block; padding: 5px; width: 237px;
  border: 1px solid #000; text-align:right}
.borderBottomLeftRight {border-left: 1px solid Black;
  border-bottom: 1px solid Black; border-right: 1px solid Black;
  font-family: Arial, Helvetica, sans-serif; font-size: 9pt;
  font-style: normal; line-height: normal; font-weight: normal;
  color: #000000; text-decoration: none;}
.borderBottomRight {font-family: Arial, Helvetica, sans-serif;
  font-size: 9pt; font-style: normal; line-height: normal;
  font-weight: normal; color: #000000; text-decoration: none;
  border-bottom: 1px solid Black; border-right: 1px solid Black;}
.borderAll {font-family: Arial, Helvetica, sans-serif; font-size: 9pt;
  font-style: normal; line-height: normal; font-weight: normal;
  color: #000000; text-decoration: none; border: 1px solid Black;}
.borderBottomLeft { font-family: Arial, Helvetica, sans-serif;
  border-bottom: 1px solid Black; border-left: 1px solid Black;
  font-size: 9pt; font-style: normal; line-height: normal;
  font-weight: normal; color: #000000; text-decoration: none;}
</style>
</head>
<body>

  <!-- page break always for printing -->
  <br style="page-break-before:always;" />
```

```
<div id="slip">

  <div id="headerLogo" style="float:left; padding-right:10px;">
    <img src="logo.png">
  </div>
  <div id="headerCompany" style="float:left">
    <H1>Your Company</H1><br/>
    yourcompany.com<br/>
    support@yourcompany.com<br/>
    1-800-852-1973
  </div>

  <div id="invoice">
    <fieldset>
      <legend>Shipping Invoice</legend>
      <ol>
        <li><label>Date</label><span><<DATE>></span></li>
        <li><label>Status</label><span><<STATUS>></span></li>
        <li><label>Txn ID</label><span><<TXNID>></span></li>
      </ol>
    </fieldset>
  </div>

  <!-- address blocks -->
  <div id="shipto">
    <fieldset>
      <legend>Ship To</legend>
      <p style="margin:5px 0px 5px 10px;"><<ADDRESS>></p>
    </fieldset>
  </div>

  <!-- order details -->
  <div style="clear:both; padding-top:50px;">
    <table width="100%" border="0px" cellpadding="0" cellspacing="0">
      <tr>
        <td colspan="4" align="left" class="borderAll">
          <p class="sliptableheader">Order Details</p>
        </td>
      </tr>
      <tr>
        <td width="12%" align="center" class="borderBottomLeftRight">
          <p class="sliptableheader">Item #</p>
        </td>
        <td align="center" class="borderBottomRight">
          <p class="sliptableheader">Item</p>
        </td>
        <td align="center" class="borderBottomRight">
          <p class="sliptableheader">Quantity</p>
        </td>
        <td width="10%" align="right" class="borderBottomRight"
            nowrap>
          <p class="sliptableheader">Ext Price</p>
```

```
      </td>
    </tr>
    <<ITEMS>>
    <tr>
      <td align="rigt" valign="top" class="borderBottomLeftRight">
      </td>
      <td align="left" valign="top" class="borderBottomRight">
        <p class="sliptabledata"> </p>
      </td>
      <td align="center" valign="top" class="borderBottomRight">
        <p class="sliptabledata"> </p>
      </td>
      <td align="center" valign="top" class="borderBottomRight">
        <p class="sliptabledata"> </p>
      </td>
    </tr>
    <tr>
      <td colspan="2" align="center" class="borderBottomLeft">
        Thank you for your order. We look forward to serving you
        in the future.
      </td>
      <td align="right" class="borderBottomRight">
        <p class="sliptabledata">
          Subtotal<br/>
          Shipping<br/>
          Handling<br/>
          Tax
        </p>
      </td>
      <td align="right" valign="top" class="borderBottomRight"
          nowrap>
        <p class="sliptabledata">
          <<SUBTOTAL>><br/>
          <<SHIPPING>><br/>
          <<HANDLING>><br/>
          <<TAX>>
        </p>
      </td>
    </tr>
    <tr>
      <td colspan="3" width="90%" align="right"
          class="borderBottomLeftRight">
        <p class="sliptableheader">Total ($ USD)</p>
      </td>
      <td width="10%" align="right" valign="top"
          class="borderBottomRight" nowrap>
        <p class="sliptableheader"><<TOTAL>>
      </td>
    </tr>
  </table>
```

```
      </div>
    </div>
  </body>
</html>
```

Now that we have the IPN listener and the template shipping invoice HTML file in place, we can send a test IPN from the PayPal sandbox. If you do not have a developer login to the sandbox, go to *https://developer.paypal.com* and create an account.

After logging into the PayPal sandbox, navigate to the Test Tools section in the site menu. On the Test Tools page, select the Instant Payment Notification (IPN) Simulator as seen in Figure 4-3.

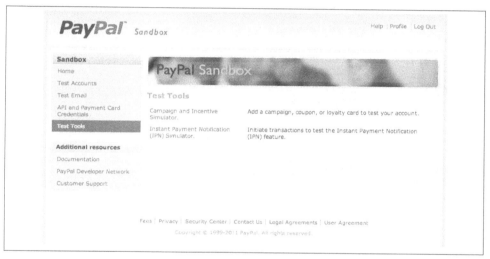

Figure 4-3. PayPal Sandbox IPN Simulator

The IPN Simulator provides prebuilt forms with the required fields for a variety of transaction types, including express checkout, cart checkout, and eBay checkout. More importantly, you can set the payment status of the transaction to test refunds, cancelled payments, and other statuses if needed.

When the IPN Simulator loads, enter the URL of your IPN listener in the *IPN Handler URL* field and select "Cart Checkout" as the transaction type. The test IPN form will open with prefilled entries where appropriate. Update any of the fields you would like, and then click "Send IPN." The simulator will refresh and inform you whether the IPN was sent successfully to the listener. If the IPN delivery failed, the IPN Simulator will typically display the reason, such as "HTTP error code 404: Not Found." Make sure that you have entered the URL of your listener correctly.

Note that IPNs sent from the IPN Simulator will include an extra key/
value pair in their payload, *test_ipn=1*, which designates that the IPN
has come from the simulator and allows you to catch test IPNs independently in your code if desired.

If the IPN delivery is successful, the resulting shipping invoice will be found in your *slips*
directory. Figure 4-4 shows how the individual fields from our test IPN have been taken
and put into the shipping invoice in their appropriate places.

Figure 4-4. Resulting shipping invoice

Remember, to put this example into production you will need to change the debug flag
in the listener to `false` to set the correct PayPal account to send IPNs to when transactions are received. You can also tell PayPal to send IPNs via a notification URL field
on individual transactions if you want to programmatically set the notification URL.

 In this example a single listener is employed to handle all IPNs that are
sent, but multiple IPN listeners can be employed to handle different
transaction types. In this manner, a different listener could handle refund transactions launched from a refund page, for example. The `noti
fication_url` field can be used in many of the PayPal API calls to des-
ignate an IPN listener.

This scenario provides a brief example of leveraging the IPN functionality built into PayPal transactions to automate your backend systems. Your specific listener could perform a number of desired functions, including customer order database updates, customer emailings, recurring payment status notifications, refund administration, and account management.

See Also

PayPal Integration Center – Introducing IPN (*https://cms.paypal.com/us/cgi-bin/? cmd=_render-content&content_ID=developer/e_howto_admin_IPNIntro*)

PayPal Developer Network Code Samples – Instant Payment Notification (*https:// www.x.com/developers/PayPal/documentation-tools/code-sample/216623*)

4.2. Simple Shipping Extension in Magento

Opportunity

Setting up a storefront is made extremely easy with the many features of Magento. One of the most powerful yet underutilized features of the Magento commerce system is the ability to customize it by adding your own extension or module. An area that people often want to enhance or add their own custom logic to is the available shipping methods. Magento covers quite a few of the standard shipping carriers, including DHL, UPS, and FedEx, but you may have your own packer/shipper or want to set up your own charging structure for different methods.

Solution

The code structure of Magento has been set up to allow for fairly straightforward extension of functionality through the addition of configuration files and PHP code. You may have a shipper with an accessible API for shipping method calculations, or want to structure your own calculated methods. With Magento, you can add the new shipping carrier or methods by adding a new module, which will automatically be picked up by Magento and integrated into the administration area and shopping cart.

Discussion

In this example a new shipping carrier module will be created for a fictitious carrier, "Rubber Ducky Shipping." The carrier offers two simple shipping methods, "slow boat" and "fast plane," as seen in the bottom of the checkout page shown in Figure 4-5.

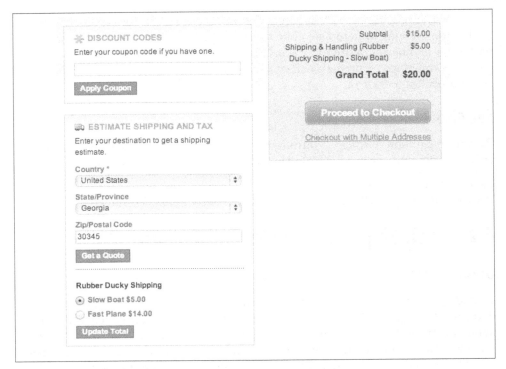

Figure 4-5. Shipping options shown on the cart

After completing the module, using the code provided as a basis you will be able to create your own version and change the shipping method logic to support your own carrier API or custom shipping methods.

To create a full shipping carrier solution, the new shipping module will also appear in the system configuration shipping methods section for setup and will automatically be pulled into the list of available shipping methods when a customer checks out with his cart. The shipping method calculations will be simple and be based on a formula of a base fee plus a percentage of the cart subtotal. You'll be able to set the fee and percentage amounts for the formula in the Magento system configuration for the shipping carrier methods. The example will be broken into the following four steps:

1. Create the Magento module directory structure.

2. Add the module definition through configuration files.

3. Add the module settings to the Magento system configuration.

4. Create the shipping method logic and validate the functionality in a cart.

The first step is to prepare the directory structure for the module configuration and logic files that will be added to define the module. In a default community installation of Magento the *app/code* directory structure will only contain *community* and *core* subdirectories, which represent the code pools used by default.

 For this example we are using the latest version of Magento Community Edition, version 1.7.0.2, with the optional sample data, version 1.6.1.0. The Magento Community Edition and sample data are available for download (*http://www.magentocommerce.com/download*).

A third code pool is available, named *local*. The local code pool is for extensions to the core code that are only for this specific, or local, instance of Magento. The local code pool will be the home for our shipping module, so we will need to add the *local* subdirectory and the child subdirectory structure, as seen in Figure 4-6.

```
▼  app
   ▼  code
      ▶  community
      ▶  core
      ▼  local
         ▼  RubberDucky
            ▼  ShippingModule
                  etc
               ▼  Model
                     Carrier
```

Figure 4-6. New module directory structure

In addition to adding the *local* subdirectory and the module subdirectories under the *local* folder, it is important to inform the PHP server about the *local* path so that Magento can find the new module. You will need to make sure that the *local* subdirectory is in the include_path variable of your PHP implementation.

 It is essential that the include_path of your PHP environment contain the *app/code/local* path so that Magento can locate and execute the module. You can verify the path contents by checking the include_path variable of the phpinfo method.

Once the directory structure is set in the Magento installation, you can define the module by adding two configuration files. The first configuration file defines the module, the current active status, and which code pool the module files may be found in. The XML configuration file is named based on your module's name; for this example it will be called *RubberDucky_ShippingModule.xml* and is shown in Example 4-3. Once you have created this file, you should copy it into the */app/etc* Magento directory.

Example 4-3. RubberDucky_ShippingModule.xml definition

```
<config>
  <modules>
    <RubberDucky_ShippingModule>
      <active>true</active>
      <codePool>local</codePool>
    </RubberDucky_ShippingModule>
  </modules>
</config>
```

The second configuration file required for the Magento system to recognize the module is *config.xml*, shown in Example 4-4. The *config.xml* file defines the version of the module, the class model to use, and the resources for the module. This file should be placed in the */app/code/local/RubberDucky/ShippingModule/etc* folder.

Example 4-4. config.xml for ShippingModule/etc folder

```
<?xml version="1.0"?>
<config>
  <modules>
    <RubberDucky_ShippingModule>
      <version>1.0.0</version>
    </RubberDucky_ShippingModule>
  </modules>
  <global>
    <models>
      <shippingmodule>
        <class>RubberDucky_ShippingModule_Model</class>
      </shippingmodule>
    </models>
    <resources>
      <shippingmodule_setup>
        <setup>
          <module>RubberDucky_ShippingModule</module>
        </setup>
        <connection>
          <use>core_setup</use>
        </connection>
      </shippingmodule_setup>
    </resources>
  </global>
  <default>
    <carriers>
      <shippingmodule>
        <active>1</active>
```

```
        <model>shippingmodule/carrier_shippingmodule</model>
      </shippingmodule>
    </carriers>
  </default>
</config>
```

Once these two configuration files are in place, the system will recognize the extension. However, we have not told the system how to present the module in the administration side of Magento or the frontend, so nothing will be seen as yet in the Magento frontend.

 If you are working on a development system, it may be easier when working with extensions and modules to turn caching off in Magento through System → Cache Management. Otherwise, as you make changes to the module you will need to flush the Magento cache to pick up the new modifications.

To enable management of the module's settings through System → Configuration → Shipping Methods in the administration area, the Magento system needs to be told what properties can be set. This is done through an XML configuration file called *sys tem.xml*, shown in Example 4-5. This file should be placed in the module *etc* directory, like the *config.xml* file (i.e., in */app/code/local/RubberDucky_ShippingModule/etc*). The purpose of this file is to define the specific settings of the module, including an active switch, title, and presentation sort order. In this case other fields are also included, which will allow the administrator to set the shipping method base fees and percentages to be used. The fields for the shipping methods are defined as slow_boat_base_fee, slow_boat_base_percent, fast_plane_base_fee, and fast_plane_base_percent. The fields defined in the *system.xml* file will be used in the logic of the module for doing the calculations we need for each shipping rate.

Example 4-5. system.xml configuration file

```
<?xml version="1.0"?>
<config>
  <sections>
    <carriers>
      <groups>
        <shippingmodule translate="label" module="shipping">
          <label>Rubber Ducky Shipping</label>
          <frontend_type>text</frontend_type>
          <sort_order>13</sort_order>
          <show_in_default>1</show_in_default>
          <show_in_website>1</show_in_website>
          <show_in_store>1</show_in_store>
          <fields>
            <active translate="label">
              <label>Enabled</label>
```

```xml
    <frontend_type>select</frontend_type>
    <source_model>
      adminhtml/system_config_source_yesno
    </source_model>
    <sort_order>1</sort_order>
    <show_in_default>1</show_in_default>
    <show_in_website>1</show_in_website>
    <show_in_store>1</show_in_store>
  </active>
  <title translate="label">
    <label>Title</label>
    <frontend_type>text</frontend_type>
    <sort_order>2</sort_order>
    <show_in_default>1</show_in_default>
    <show_in_website>1</show_in_website>
    <show_in_store>1</show_in_store>
  </title>
  <slow_boat_base_fee translate="label">
    <label>Slow boat base fee</label>
    <frontend_type>text</frontend_type>
    <sort_order>10</sort_order>
    <show_in_default>1</show_in_default>
    <show_in_website>1</show_in_website>
    <show_in_store>1</show_in_store>
  </slow_boat_base_fee>
  <slow_boat_percent translate="label">
    <label>Slow boat percent add (0.05 = 5 percent)</label>
    <frontend_type>text</frontend_type>
    <sort_order>11</sort_order>
    <show_in_default>1</show_in_default>
    <show_in_website>1</show_in_website>
    <show_in_store>1</show_in_store>
  </slow_boat_percent>
  <fast_plane_base_fee translate="label">
    <label>Fast plane base fee</label>
    <frontend_type>text</frontend_type>
    <sort_order>12</sort_order>
    <show_in_default>1</show_in_default>
    <show_in_website>1</show_in_website>
    <show_in_store>1</show_in_store>
  </fast_plane_base_fee>
  <fast_plane_percent translate="label">
    <label>Fast plane percent add (0.15 = 15 percent)</label>
    <frontend_type>text</frontend_type>
    <sort_order>13</sort_order>
    <show_in_default>1</show_in_default>
    <show_in_website>1</show_in_website>
    <show_in_store>1</show_in_store>
  </fast_plane_percent>
  <specificerrmsg translate="label">
    <label>Displayed Error Message</label>
    <frontend_type>textarea</frontend_type>
```

```
              <sort_order>80</sort_order>
              <show_in_default>1</show_in_default>
              <show_in_website>1</show_in_website>
              <show_in_store>1</show_in_store>
            </specificerrmsg>
            <showmethod translate="label">
              <label>Show method if not applicable</label>
              <frontend_type>select</frontend_type>
              <sort_order>92</sort_order>
              <source_model>
                adminhtml/system_config_source_yesno
              </source_model>
              <show_in_default>1</show_in_default>
              <show_in_website>1</show_in_website>
              <show_in_store>1</show_in_store>
            </showmethod>
            <sort_order translate="label">
              <label>Sort order</label>
              <frontend_type>text</frontend_type>
              <sort_order>100</sort_order>
              <show_in_default>1</show_in_default>
              <show_in_website>1</show_in_website>
              <show_in_store>1</show_in_store>
            </sort_order>
          </fields>
        </shippingmodule>
      </groups>
    </carriers>
  </sections>
</config>
```

If you review the other shipping carriers in the Magento shipping methods configuration area, you will find many other fields that could be added. The fields that you add will be determined by what your logic requires. For example, if your shipping calculations leverage an outside API set that requires a set of credentials, your settings may include fields for the remote service login credentials.

> If you'd like to see the *system.xml* definition files for some of the other shipping carriers, the default *system.xml* for the included carriers is available at *app/code/core/Mage/Usa/etc/system.xml*. This file includes the shipping carrier properties for all the out-of-box services, such as FedEx and UPS.

After uploading the *config.xml* file to the proper location, you can verify that Magento has loaded the module and the settings are available by logging into the administration side of Magento and navigating to the System → Configuration → Shipping Methods area. If the module has been configured correctly, you should see the Rubber Ducky Shipping carrier listed among the possible carriers, with the settings defined in the *config.xml* file (as seen in Figure 4-7).

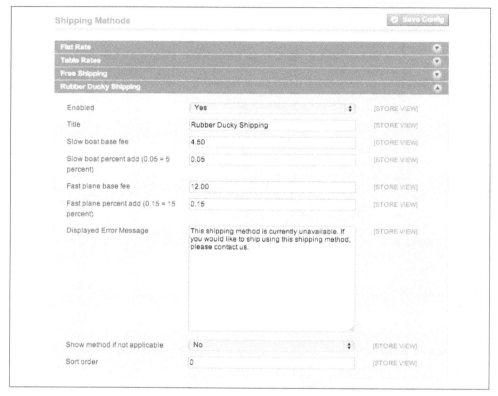

Figure 4-7. The shipping module in Magento's shipping methods configuration area

When you open the Rubber Ducky Shipping carrier settings the first time, the values for the properties will be empty. The *Enabled* field should be set to *Yes* and the title to the name of the carrier. The base fee and percentage can be filled in with the values you would like to be used for your calculations. Here, the values $4.50 and 5 percent and $12.00 and 15 percent have been used for the slow boat and fast plane methods, respectively. A text block can be added for display when an error occurs, and you can select to hide the method if not applicable. Lastly, to give the carrier top billing in the list of carriers displayed in the cart, set the sort order to zero. Click "Save Config" to save the settings. The module settings should now be configured.

Now that the module has been configured in the administration console, the last step is to add the logic for doing the actual calculations for our two shipping methods, slow boat and fast plane. To add the logic for the new module, we have to add the shipping module class PHP file into the */app/code/local/RubberDucky/ShippingModule/Model/ Carrier* directory. The name of the file will be *Shippingmodule.php*, and the contents are shown in Example 4-6.

 The naming scheme for a module is required to be consistent throughout the configuration files, directory structure, and class file. This is how Magento will locate your class file and module definitions. The actual names used in this example are for demonstration purposes and can be replaced by your own names, as long as they are consistent throughout. If the naming is not consistent, Magento will not be able to properly load and execute your module class, resulting in system errors.

Example 4-6. Shippingmodule.php

```php
<?php
/**
 * Shippingmodule.php
 *
 * PHP file for implementing the new shipping model in the cart
 * and checkout.
 *
 * @method RubberDucky_ShippingModule_Model_Carrier_Shippingmodule
 *    collectRates(Mage_Shipping_Model_Rate_Request $request)
 * @method array getAllowedMethods()
 *
 * @author       Chuck Hudson
 */

class RubberDucky_ShippingModule_Model_Carrier_Shippingmodule extends
  Mage_Shipping_Model_Carrier_Abstract {

  /**
   * Code of the carrier
   *
   * @var string
   */
  const CODE = 'shippingmodule';

  /**
   * Code of the carrier
   *
   * @var string
   */
  protected $_code = self::CODE;
```

```
/**
 * Collect the rates for this shipping method to display.
 *
 * @param Mage_Shipping_Model_Rate_Request $request
 * @return Mage_Shipping_Model_Rate_Result
 */
public function collectRates(Mage_Shipping_Model_Rate_Request
  $request) {

  // Return now if this carrier is not active in the configured
  // shipping methods.
  if (!Mage::getStoreConfig('carriers/'.$this->_code.'/active')) {
    return false;
  }

  // Create the container for holding rates for this shipping method.
  $result = Mage::getModel('shipping/rate_result');

  // Get shipping method settings (base fee and percentage add
  // of subtotal).
  $slow_boat_base_fee = Mage::getStoreConfig('carriers/'.$this-
    >_code.'/slow_boat_base_fee');
  $slow_boat_percent = Mage::getStoreConfig('carriers/'.$this-
    >_code.'/slow_boat_percent');
  $fast_plane_base_fee = Mage::getStoreConfig('carriers/'.$this-
    >_code.'/fast_plane_base_fee');
  $fast_plane_percent = Mage::getStoreConfig('carriers/'.$this-
    >_code.'/fast_plane_percent');

  // Retrieve cart subtotal for calculating additional percentage.
  $subtotal = $this->_getCartSubtotal();

  // Calculate "Slow Boat" method rate and append to the collection.
  $rate = Mage::getModel('shipping/rate_result_method');
  $rate->setCarrier($this->_code);
  $rate->setCarrierTitle($this->getConfigData('title'));
  $rate->setMethod('slowboat');
  $rate->setMethodTitle('Slow Boat');
  $rate->setCost($slow_boat_base_fee);
  $rate->setPrice(number_format($slow_boat_base_fee+
    ($subtotal*$slow_boat_percent)),2);
  $result->append($rate);

  // Calculate "Fast Plane" method rate and append to the collection.
  $rate = Mage::getModel('shipping/rate_result_method');
  $rate->setCarrier($this->_code);
  $rate->setCarrierTitle($this->getConfigData('title'));
  $rate->setMethod('fastplane');
  $rate->setMethodTitle('Fast Plane');
  $rate->setCost($fast_plane_base_fee);
  $rate->setPrice(number_format($fast_plane_base_fee+
    ($subtotal*$fast_plane_percent)),2);
```

```
    $result->append($rate);

    // Return the collection of shipping rates for display.
    return $result;
}

/**
 * Get order subtotal
 *
 * @return float
 */
protected function _getCartSubtotal() {
    // Retrieve the totals of the current cart.
    $cartTotals =
        Mage::getSingleton('checkout/cart')->getQuote()->getTotals();
    // Get the subtotal value from the totals array.
    $cartSubtotal = $cartTotals["subtotal"]->getValue();
    return $cartSubtotal;
}

/**
 * Get allowed shipping methods
 *
 * @return array
 */
public function getAllowedMethods() {
    return array($this->_code => $this->getConfigData('name'));
}
}
?>
```

The *Shippingmodule.php* file defines the class for the RubberDucky_ShippingMod
ule_Model_Carrier_Shippingmodule module, and the class name follows the subdirectory structure. Inside the module logic class are two functions that are required for
working with shipping methods, the getAllowedMethods and collectRates functions.
The getAllowedMethods function simply informs Magento of the allowed methods. The
collectRates function is called from the cart and checkout process to "collect the rates"
for the different shipping methods of this carrier. In this case the logic is fairly simple:
it requires the retrieval of the shipping method fee and percentage to be used from the
stored configuration data that was set in the administration console. The code will
retrieve the current cart subtotal via a helper function, _getCartSubtotal. The values
are then used to calculate the slow boat rate and the fast plane rate, which are added to
the result object. The result object is then returned to the caller of the class for display,
as shown in Figure 4-8.

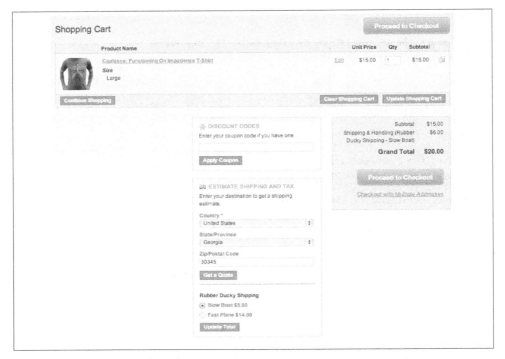

Figure 4-8. Completed shipping option in cart

This example has shown an easy way to add your own shipping module into a Magento installation. The shipping methods used here are quite simple, but the logic and calculations can be replaced with your own matrix of calculations, or rates calculated through a remote service and looped through to add them to the result to be displayed in the cart or checkout. This can be a powerful way to customize the shipping experience for your customers.

See Also

Magento Connect – Create Your Extension (*http://bit.ly/V3IIf0*)

Magento Connect Extension Developer's Guidelines (*http://bit.ly/ZgQCKL*)

4.3. Multiple Supplier Fulfillment

Opportunity

For many product-based businesses, the inventory or goods they sell may be sourced from multiple suppliers that can ship directly to customers. An opportunity exists to minimize inventory on hand, expedite customer shipments, and automate processing if product suppliers can be paid at the time of sale. The profit margin can remain with the seller while the suppliers can ship the goods when they are paid. In essence, one primary receiver of the funds exists from the buyer's viewpoint, and the funds are then split accordingly among other receivers.

Solution

In this scenario a customer chooses a range of products and completes the purchase at company XYZ's online store. When the purchase is made, the customer pays company XYZ the total amount. Behind the scenes, the funds are automatically split between company XYZ and the other companies that are supplying the products the customer has selected. For example, two products may come from company XYZ, while two come from company A and the fifth product from company B. The payment is automatically split among these companies based on the costs negotiated in a "chained payment," as shown in Figure 4-9.

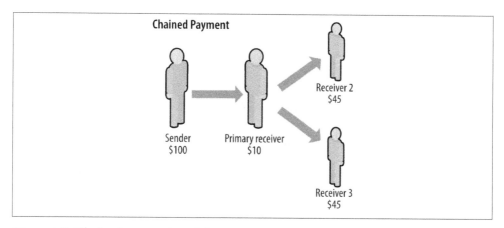

Figure 4-9. Chained payment model

The PayPal Adaptive Payments API and SDK (*https://www.x.com/developers/paypal/documentation-tools/paypal-sdk-index#adaptivepayments*) make this scenario easy to implement through a robust set of chained payment functionality. In a single API call, a payment can be sent to a primary receiver and then separate amounts passed on to other designated receivers.

 If you want to use the Adaptive Payments API in a production environment, PayPal must preapprove your PayPal account and application for security purposes.

Discussion

For this example a rudimentary order form will be used to trigger the chained payment processing. On the order form we will include an extra field, *Receiver*, which represents the supplier of the item that is being ordered and will not be shown to a normal viewer. This field will be used in the processing to determine how much money is passed on to the specific suppliers. In a production environment this information will be stored with the products in your database. A receiver ID of 0 represents our store, so we will need to take into account cases where goods are coming directly from us. Figure 4-10 shows the order form as displayed from *orderForm.php*.

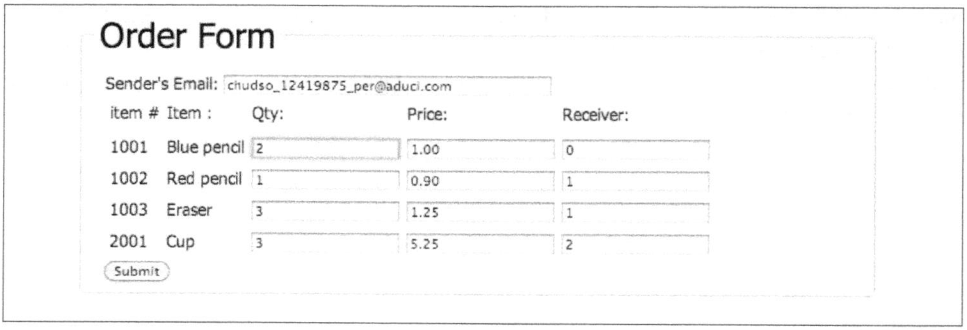

Order Form

Sender's Email: `chudso_12419875_per@aduci.com`

item #	Item :	Qty:	Price:	Receiver:
1001	Blue pencil	2	1.00	0
1002	Red pencil	1	0.90	1
1003	Eraser	3	1.25	1
2001	Cup	3	5.25	2

Submit

Figure 4-10. Basic order form with receiver ID

In Example 4-7 you can see the HTML behind the order form, which includes additional hidden fields for each item. The input values are structured as arrays so that the PHP page to which the form is posted can loop through the items. This shopping cart experience would normally be implemented with a database and session variables, but it is simplified here to show the process for setting up and kicking off a chained payment using the Adaptive Payments API.

Example 4-7. orderForm.php

```php
<?php
/************************************************************
orderForm.php

Sample order form that kicks off chained payment. In practice
this would be your shopping cart checkout page.

Calls processOrder.php from form submittal.

************************************************************/
?>

<!DOCTYPE html>
<html>
```

```
<head>
<title>Order Form - Chained Payments</title>
<style>
* {margin: 0; padding: 0;}
body {background: #fff; color: #000;
  font: normal 90%/1.5 tahoma, verdana, sans-serif;}
h1 {font-size: 2.9em; font-weight: bold; margin: 1em 0 1em 10px;}
form {padding: 0 10px; width: 700px;}
legend {font-size: 2em; padding-left: 5px; padding-right: 5px;
  position: relative;}
fieldset {border: 1px solid #ccc; border-radius: 5px; float: left;
  padding: 10px; width: 640px;}
td {padding: 2px;}
</style>
</head>
<body>
<div id="orderForm">
<fieldset>
  <legend>Order Form</legend>
  <form id="orderForm" name="orderForm"action="processOrder.php"
    method="post">
  <div>
    Sender's Email: <input type="text" size="50" maxlength="64"
      name="email" placeholder="Sandbox account email"
      value="chudso_1241987592_per@aduci.com">
  </div>
  <table align="center">
    <thead>
      <tr>
        <td>item #</td>
        <td>Item :</td>
        <td>Qty:</td>
        <td>Price:</td>
        <td>Receiver:</td>
      </tr>
    </thead>
    <tr>
      <td><input type="hidden" name="item[]" value="1001" />1001</td>
      <td>Blue pencil</td>
      <td><input type="text" name="qty[]" value="2" /></td>
      <td><input type="text" name="price[]" value="1.00" /></td>
      <td><input type="text" name="source[]" value="0" /></td>
    </tr>
    <tr>
      <td><input type="hidden" name="item[]" value="1002" />1002</td>
      <td>Red pencil</td>
      <td><input type="text" name="qty[]" value="1" /></td>
      <td><input type="text" name="price[]" value="0.90" /></td>
      <td><input type="text" name="source[]" value="1" /></td>
    </tr>
    <tr>
      <td><input type="hidden" name="item[]" value="1003" />1003</td>
```

```
    <td>Eraser</td>
    <td><input type="text" name="qty[]" value="3" /></td>
    <td><input type="text" name="price[]" value="1.25" /></td>
    <td><input type="text" name="source[]" value="1" /></td>
  </tr>
  <tr>
    <td><input type="hidden" name="item[]" value="2001" />2001</td>
    <td>Cup</td>
    <td><input type="text" name="qty[]" value="3" /></td>
    <td><input type="text" name="price[]" value="5.25" /></td>
    <td><input type="text" name="source[]" value="2" /></td>
  </tr>
  </table>
  <div><input type="submit" value="Submit" /></div>
  </form>
</fieldset>
</div>
</body>
</html>
```

When submitted, the order form is posted to a processing page, *processOrder.php*, that will process the items and execute the Adaptive Payments `Pay` call. The processing page will leverage a code library from the PayPal Adaptive Payments SDK. The SDK provides a production-ready framework and examples on which you can base your Adaptive Payments solutions.

Once you have downloaded the SDK for Adaptive Payments (*https://www.x.com/devel opers/paypal/documentation-tools/paypal-sdk-index#adaptivepayments*) from the X.com developer site, place the *lib* folder in the same location as the order form and the new *processOrder.php* page, which will be created shortly.

 The *processOrder.php*, *APIError.php*, and *PaymentDetails.php* pages are based on files that are included in the *samples* folder of the Adaptive Payments SDK. The *samples* folder also includes examples of other uses of the Adaptive Payments API.

Figure 4-11 shows the process flow that we will end up with. The order form on the site will post items in the cart to the processing page, which will call the PayPal Adaptive Payments API. Depending on the PayPal payments method, on success the API may direct the user to the payment details, or return the API results to the processing page. If there is a failure in the API call, the API error page will be shown. The customer may also cancel the PayPal transaction during the process, which will bring her back to the order form.

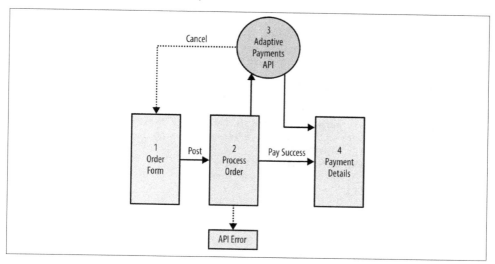

Figure 4-11. Chained payment flow

The *processOrder.php* page has been modified from a copy of the *payChained Receipt.php* page found in the SDK samples. The new page will perform the following steps:

1. Set the endpoint for the API calls.
2. Create a `PayRequest` message envelope.
3. Create the receiver list for the payments.
4. Set any optional `PayRequest` fields.
5. Execute the `Pay` API call with the `PayRequest`.
6. Check the results of the call and redirect the page accordingly.

The complete *processOrder.php* is included in Example 4-8.

Example 4-8. processOrder.php

```php
<?php
/***********************************************
processOrder.php

Called by orderForm.php.
Calls  APIError.php on error.

Based on PayChainedReceipt.php from SDK samples.
***********************************************/

require_once 'lib/AdaptivePayments.php';
require_once 'web_constants.php';
```

```php
session_start();

try {

  /* The servername and serverport tell PayPal where the buyer
     should be directed back to after authorizing payment. In this
     case, it's the local web server that is running this script. Using
     the servername and serverport, the return URL is the first portion
     of the URL that buyers will return to after authorizing payment.*/
  $serverName = $_SERVER['SERVER_NAME'];
  $serverPort = $_SERVER['SERVER_PORT'];
  $url=dirname('http://'.$serverName.':'.$serverPort.
    $_SERVER['REQUEST_URI']);

  /* The returnURL is the location where buyers return when a
     payment has been succesfully authorized. The cancelURL is
     the location buyers are sent to when they hit the cancel
     button during authorization of payment during the PayPal flow.*/
  $returnURL = $url."/PaymentDetails.php";
  $cancelURL = "$url/orderForm.php" ;
  $email = $_REQUEST["email"];

  /* Set a couple of arrays of item costs and receivers, since we
     are not using a real database in this example. Normally this
     information would come from the shopping cart and/or database
     being used to track items being sold and sources.*/
  $arrItemCosts = array('1001' => 1.00,
    '1002' => 0.60,
    '1003' => 1.00,
    '2001' => 4.00);

  // Set array of receivers with us first (based on order).
  $arrReceivers = array('wppm_1341107399_biz@aduci.com',
    'sell1_1341107573_biz@aduci.com',
    'servic_1241987644_biz@aduci.com');
  $arrReceiverAmounts = array();

  // Determine and set amounts for each receiver.
  $totalSale = 0;

  $itemCount = count($_POST['item']);
  for ($idxItem=0; $idxItem<$itemCount; $idxItem++) {

    /* Get each item's data. This would typically come
       from the cart/database.*/
    $itemSku = $_POST['item'][$idxItem];
    $itemQty = $_POST['qty'][$idxItem];
    $itemSource = $_POST['source'][$idxItem];
    $itemPrice = $_POST['price'][$idxItem];
    $itemCost = $arrItemCosts[$itemSku];
```

```php
    // Update total sale amount.
    $totalSale += $itemQty * $itemPrice;

    // Calculate amount for this item and add to receiver amounts.
    $itemAmount = $itemQty * $itemCost;
    $arrReceiverAmounts[$itemSource] += $itemAmount;
}


// Set the total sale to our own primary receiver.
$arrReceiverAmounts[0] += $totalSale;

/* Make the call to PayPal to get the Pay token.
   If the API call succeeded, then redirect the buyer to PayPal
   to begin to authorize payment. If an error occurred, show the
   resulting errors.*/
$payRequest = new PayRequest();
$payRequest->actionType = "PAY";
$payRequest->cancelUrl = $cancelURL ;
$payRequest->returnUrl = $returnURL;
$payRequest->clientDetails = new ClientDetailsType();
$payRequest->clientDetails->applicationId = APPLICATION_ID;
$payRequest->clientDetails->deviceId = DEVICE_ID;
$payRequest->clientDetails->ipAddress = "127.0.0.1";
$payRequest->currencyCode = "USD";
$payRequest->senderEmail = $email;
$payRequest->requestEnvelope = new RequestEnvelope();
$payRequest->requestEnvelope->errorLanguage = "en_US";

// Set the receivers.
$arrReceiverList = array();

for ($idxReceivers=0; $idxReceivers<count($arrReceivers);
  $idxReceivers++) {

  $tmpReceiver = new receiver();
  $tmpReceiver->email = $arrReceivers[$idxReceivers];
  $tmpReceiver->amount = $arrReceiverAmounts[$idxReceivers];
  if ($idxReceivers == 0) {
    // If receiver is us, set primary to true.
    $tmpReceiver->primary = true;
  } else {
    $tmpReceiver->primary = false;
  }

  // Create a unique invoice per receiver (replace with yours).
  $tmpReceiver->invoiceId = "12009-" . $idxReceivers;

  // Add this receiver to the array.
  array_push($arrReceiverList, $tmpReceiver);
}

// Set the array of receivers into the Pay Request.
```

```php
    $payRequest->receiverList = $arrReceiverList;

    // Set optional Pay Request fields.
    $payRequest->feesPayer = "EACHRECEIVER";
    $payRequest->memo = "Chained Payment";

    /* Make the call to PayPal to get the Pay token.
       If the API call succeeded, then redirect the buyer to PayPal
       to begin to authorize payment. If an error occurred, show the
       resulting errors.*/
    $ap = new AdaptivePayments();
    $response=$ap->Pay($payRequest);

    if (strtoupper($ap->isSuccess) == 'FAILURE') {
      $_SESSION['FAULTMSG']=$ap->getLastError();
      $location = "APIError.php";
      header("Location: $location");
    } else {
      $_SESSION['payKey'] = $response->payKey;
      if ($response->paymentExecStatus == "COMPLETED") {
        $location = "PaymentDetails.php";
        header("Location: $location");
      } else {
        $token = $response->payKey;
        $payPalURL = PAYPAL_REDIRECT_URL.'_ap-payment&paykey='.$token;
        header("Location: ".$payPalURL);
      }
    }
}
catch(Exception $ex) {
  $fault = new FaultMessage();
  $errorData = new ErrorData();
  $errorData->errorId = $ex->getFile();
  $errorData->message = $ex->getMessage();
  $fault->error = $errorData;
  $_SESSION['FAULTMSG']=$fault;
  $location = "APIError.php";
  header("Location: $location");
}
?>
```

In the *processOrder.php* page, the key difference from a normal PayPal transaction is the creation of a list of receivers. The list of receivers is added to the `PayRequest` to tell the API method who the primary and secondary receivers are and the appropriate amounts to transfer to each. In this example the script will cycle through the list of items ordered and add to each receiver's amount the wholesale cost of the item multiplied by the quantity. The item costs are pulled from an embedded array, `$arrItemCosts`, but normally this information would be pulled from your product database or be available in the shopping cart with other item information.

The script marks the account of the first receiver, which represents the storefront, as the primary receiver. This receiver will be the initial recipient of all funds, so the total order amount must be set as the amount for this receiver. PayPal will automatically transfer from the primary receiver the designated amounts for the other receivers.

 The primary receiver's amount set for the transaction must be equal to or greater than the amounts of all receivers combined, or the payment transaction will fail.

To allow for easier identification of the amounts for each receiver, the script also adds an optional invoice ID with a unique extension for each receiver. You will want to generate the invoice IDs dynamically in your own solution.

 In a chained payment, PayPal allows a maximum of five receivers to be designated in one request.

After adding the array of receivers to the pay request, the script sets some optional parameters for the payment. A field titled feesPayer instructs PayPal which model to use for charging transaction fees for the chained payment. In this case the value of EACHRECEIVER is used to signify that each receiver will pay a proportional amount of the total fees for its received monies. Two other options for fee payment are available: PRIMARYRECEIVER signifies that the primary receiver will pay all fees, while SECONDARYONLY designates that the secondary receiver will pay all fees when only one secondary receiver is included.

The second field, memo, is for any memo that you would like to be added with the transaction. The memo field will be shown to the payer upon checkout and has a limit of 1,000 characters.

 In Recipe 4.1, "Just-in-Time Shipping Forms", we specified the URL for our IPN listener in the PayPal IPN Simulator. In the Pay request we can also add an optional field, ipnNotificationUrl, to designate an IPN listener for the chained payment transaction.

To run this example we will need a couple of supporting files: *web_constants.php*, which has the PayPal service endpoints defined and should not need to be changed from the version in the SDK *samples* directory; *PaymentDetails.php*, which is the landing page to which a user is sent after a successful payment; and *APIError.php*, which is used to display any errors that occur while calling the API. The files used in this example are direct copies from the SDK *samples* folder, with the links modified for the locations of the *web_constants.php* file (Example 4-9) and the *lib* folder.

Example 4-9. web_constants.php

```php
<?php
/*****************************************************
web_constants.php

Define constants used by web pages in this file.
*****************************************************/

/* Define the PayPal URL. This is the URL that the buyer is
   first sent to to authorize payment with his PayPal account.
   Change the URL depending on whether you are testing in the
   sandbox or going to the live PayPal site.
   For the sandbox, the URL is:
   https://www.sandbox.paypal.com/webscr&cmd=_ap-payment&paykey=.
   For the live site, the URL is:
   https://www.paypal.com/webscr&cmd=_ap-payment&paykey=.
   */

define('PAYPAL_REDIRECT_URL',
  'https://www.sandbox.paypal.com/webscr&cmd=');
define('DEVELOPER_PORTAL', 'https://developer.paypal.com');
define('DEVICE_ID', 'PayPal_Platform_PHP_SDK');
define('APPLICATION_ID', 'APP-80W284485P519543T');
?>
```

To test the chained payment, we will use buyer and seller accounts created in the PayPal sandbox (*https://developer.paypal.com*). In your sandbox account, create four accounts: a personal buyer account and three business seller accounts. Take the email addresses generated for the seller accounts and place them in the $arrReceivers array in the *processOrder.php* page, with the first one being your primary receiver. Lastly, put the personal buyer email address in your *orderForm.php* for the input value of "Sender's Email."

Now that the accounts are set, you can launch *orderForm.php* in a browser. Confirm that the sender's email matches the one generated in the PayPal sandbox and click "Submit." When submitted, the process order page should handle the form post and redirect to the PayPal sandbox for payment completion, as seen in Figure 4-12.

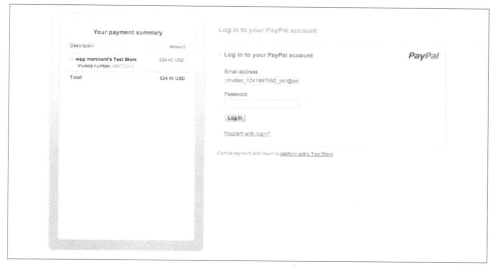

Figure 4-12. PayPal payment login

Once the PayPal payment is complete, the customer is brought to the payment details page seen in Figure 4-13, showing the debug information. You can easily substitute a receipt or other landing page for a successful payment.

Transaction ID:	0A573319X3529930V
Transaction Status:	COMPLETED
Pay Key:	AP-29913346UW634464U
Sender Email:	chudso_1241987592_per@aduci.com
Action Type:	PAY
Fees Payer:	EACHRECEIVER
Currency Code:	USD
Preapproval Key:	Not Applicable

Figure 4-13. Payment details page

In this example we have seen how easy it is to set up chained payments, where a buyer interacts with a single seller but the funds are split between different suppliers. In this case the payment has taken place immediately. The Adaptive Payments API also allows for holding payment to secondary receivers for up to 90 days. To hold the payment to secondary receivers, change the action type in the request to PAY_PRIMARY. This can allow for goods to be paid for upon receipt. Chained payments have been designed to fit a variety of buyer-to-seller-to-seller business models.

See Also

PayPal Adaptive Payments Developer Guide (*https://cms.paypal.com/cms_content/US/en_US/files/developer/PP_AdaptivePayments.pdf*)

PayPal Adaptive Payments SDK (*https://www.x.com/developers/paypal/documentation-tools/paypal-sdk-index#adaptivepayments*)

PayPal Developer Network – Pay API Operation (*https://www.x.com/developers/paypal/documentation-tools/api/pay-api-operation*)

4.4. Conclusion

The examples shown in this chapter provide a glimpse of what can be done to automate and streamline the fulfillment step of the commerce lifecycle, for the benefit of both the merchant and the consumer. Instant Payment Notifications allow you to keep your customer information databases up-to-date, know when payments have cleared, and take care of transactions that fall outside of the normal payment flow (reversals, refunds, etc.). The Magento extension shows how easy it is to customize your shipping options and provide shipping algorithms for your customers based on your specific needs. Instead of making a set of prescribed shipping options match your product orders, you can now customize those options to fit your business. Lastly, product fulfillment can leverage new payment models such as chained payments to allow product manufacturers to easily fulfill orders from other sites.

With these and other APIs the fulfillment process can be automated and integrated, shortening the time to ship, reducing shipping errors, expediting payments to vendors, and encouraging customers to come back and buy from sellers again.

CHAPTER 5

Consumption and Sharing

The last stage in the simplified commerce lifecycle (Figure 5-1) is the consumption and sharing of the product or service by the customer. In this stage customers are developing their overall perception of what they have purchased and discussing it with friends in their social circles. The time window for this stage typically starts when the customer receives the product or begins using the service purchased, although the sharing of a product purchasing experience could begin even earlier in the cycle. In either case, it is important for vendors to realize that during this stage, customers can be the best source for driving future sales and new revolutions of the commerce lifecycle.

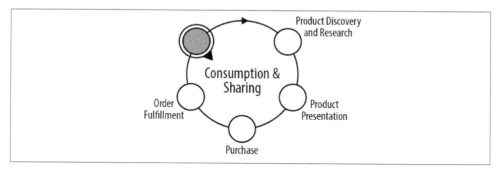

Figure 5-1. Simplified commerce lifecycle—stage 5

In many cases, this stage—in keeping with its place in the commerce lifecycle—is thought of last. Little investment may be made in improving the customer's consumption and sharing of a product. However, with some effort and simple API incorporation, this stage can quickly become a high-quality gear in the engine producing future leads and sales. This chapter will focus on two aspects of customer sharing: enabling sharing with technology and using APIs to create targeted social recommendations.

5.1. Sharing with QR Codes

Opportunity

One of the primary ways consumers share product favorites is word of mouth. For a vendor, there is no sales aid as powerful as a passionate consumer. With the social web and smartphones, consumers can easily share product likes among their social circles —and by supporting newer technologies such as Quick Response (QR) codes and scanning apps to link information about a product to a small symbol, we can make this even easier.

Solution

Typically, writing a review for a product or sharing a product with a friend requires several steps by the consumer. The process may involve the consumer searching for the item online, copying a link, and either posting it in her social feed or emailing the link to a friend. In this example we will use a QR code and the RedLaser SDK (*http://redlas er.com/developers*) to create a simple way for consumers to share product information. Users will be able to scan a code found on a product with their smart devices and be taken to a landing page in their web browsers, through which they can quickly submit the product to their favorite social feed or email product information to a friend.

Discussion

The concept of sharing a product with friends via a QR code is gaining traction, and you may have already seen the use of QR codes in stores to "tell a friend" about a product (such as in the "I LIKE DIESEL" campaign (*http://bit.ly/TY6x9k*)). However, for a lot of consumers, the "like" or "dislike" stage does not happen until they have used the product in their own environment after purchase. This example will show how to programmatically create a QR code tied to a specific product, which can be screen-printed onto a product or included on a card contained in the packaging. With the QR code can be a brief message instructing the consumer to scan the QR code to easily share the product recommendation with their friends.

 A Quick Response code is a two-dimensional barcode that can be scanned by most mobile barcode scanning applications and can contain a maximum of 4,296 encoded alphanumeric characters, based on the size and level of error correction chosen. QR codes can contain actionable links such as URLs to be opened in a browser, or *mailto:* links to open a new email by default. For more information on QR codes and their encoding and decoding, see the Wikipedia page (*http://en.wikipe dia.org/wiki/QR_code*).

To scan a QR code the consumer can use a scanning application or a custom vendor mobile application leveraging the RedLaser SDK for scanning, as we will see in this example. Once scanned, the encoded URL in the QR code will open a URL in the user's browser that will log the use of the QR code for analytics and then forward the user to a page where he can choose one of several social services by which to share the product (see Figure 5-2).

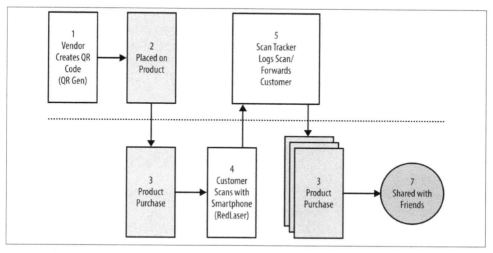

Figure 5-2. Product sharing flow via QR codes

This example is broken down into three steps:

1. Programmatic creation of a product QR code
2. Creation of an iPhone application for scanning the code
3. Presenting the appropriate page for sharing the product

The first step of this example is to create the QR code with the specific link to open when scanned. The link will pass the product ID so that the browser page presented can include specific product information. There are multiple QR code encoding libraries available, supporting various languages. One of the easiest methods for creating a code is to use the Google Infographics API. This API creates a static QR code image based on information passed in on the API call. Documentation on QR codes with the Google Infographics API is available at *https://google-developers.appspot.com/chart/infographics/docs/qr_codes*.

As of April 20, 2012, Google has deprecated the infographics part of the Google Chart Tools. Based on the Google Deprecation Policy, the API will be available through April 20, 2015. Currently the Google API for creating a QR code is possibly the easiest to integrate, but other libraries are available, including PHP QR Code (*http://phpqrcode.source forge.net/*) and QR-Generator-PHP (*https://github.com/edent/QR-Generator-PHP/*) for PHP.

To make it easy to create a specific product QR code, this example will first ask the vendor for the specific product ID to be encoded with the link, as seen in Figure 5-3.

Figure 5-3. QRShareIt.php, our QR code label entry form

The code for the QR code creation form is shown in Example 5-1. This step could be replaced with a script to automatically generate several codes from a database of products, if needed.

Example 5-1. QRShareIt.php, QR code creation form with product ID

```php
<?php
/**************************************************************
QRShareIt.php

Simple form for entering product ID for QR code referral link.

Calls QRCreateLabel.php from form submittal.

**************************************************************/
?>

<!DOCTYPE html>
<html>
<head>
<title>QR Code Creation Form</title>
<style>
* {margin: 0; padding: 0;}
body {background: #fff; color: #000;
  font: normal 62.5%/1.5 tahoma, verdana, sans-serif;}
```

```
form {padding: 0 10px; width: 700px;}
legend {font-size: 2em; padding-left: 5px; padding-right: 5px;
  position: relative;}
fieldset {border: 1px solid #ccc; border-radius: 5px; float: left;
  padding: 10px; width: 320px;}
li {clear: both; list-style-type: none; margin: 0 0 10px;}
label, input {font-size: 1.3em;}
label {display: block; padding: 0 0 5px; width: 200px}
input {background-position: 295px 5px; background-repeat: no-repeat;
  border: 2px solid #ccc; border-radius: 5px;
  padding: 5px 25px 5px 5px; width: 285px;}
input:focus {outline: none;}
input:invalid:required {background-image: url(images/asterisk.png);
  box-shadow: none;}
input:focus:invalid {background-image: url(images/invalid.png);
  box-shadow: 0px 0px 5px #b01212; border: 2px solid #b01212;}
input:valid:required {background-image: url(images/accept.png);
  border: 2px solid #7ab526;}
div {clear: both; float: left; margin: 10px 0; text-align: center;
  width: 100%;}
input[type=submit] {background: #7ab526; border: none;
  box-shadow: 0px 0px 5px #7ab526; color: #fff; cursor: pointer;
  font-size: 2em; font-weight: bold; margin: 10px auto;
  padding: 10px; width: auto;}
input[type=submit]:hover {box-shadow: 0px 0px 25px #7ab526; }
</style>
</head>
<body>
  <form id="qrForm" name="qrForm" action="QRCreateLabel.php"
    method="post">
  <fieldset>
    <legend>Create the Product QR Label</legend>
    <ol>
      <li>
        <label for="product_id">Product ID/SKU</label>
        <input type="text" id="product_id" name="product_id"
          required />
      </li>
    </ol>
    <div><input type="submit" value="Submit" /></div>
  </fieldset>
  </form>
</body>
</html>
```

When you submit the form with the product ID on the *QRShareIt.php* page, the *QRCrea teLabel.php* page (Example 5-2) will take the product ID, combine it with the landing page URL, and create an appropriate label layout, including the QR code graphic. The page will add the product ID as a query string parameter to the landing URL we have selected, which in this case is *<yoursite>.com/QRscan.php*.

For additional security, a GUID or other unique identifier could be added to the query string to authenticate the scan and product ID received.

The URL that is created will be passed to the Google API as the data to be encoded in the QR code. Next, the page creates the image source URL, which references the QR code generator at Google. The URL contains the chart type, *cht=qr*, and size, *chs=220x220*, of the image to be created. The link for the QR code is added as the *chl* query string variable. A sample URL for the QR code image generator would be:

> https://chart.googleapis.com/chart?cht=qr&chs=220x220&chl= http%3A%2F %2Fwww.%3Cyoursite%3E.com%2FQRscan.php%26pid%3DMSA2012

Notice that the example contains a link that has been encoded. The Google API will decode the passed data and include the link in the resulting QR code appropriately.

The page that handles all of this, *QRCreateLabel.php*, is shown in Example 5-2.

Example 5-2. QRCreateLabel.php, QR code creation page

```php
<?php
/*****************************************************
QRCreateLabel.php

Create the QR code label for putting on the product.

Call from QRShareIt.php with the product ID.

*****************************************************/

// For documentation on the Google QR Code Infographics API, see:
// https://google-developers.appspot.com/chart/infographics/docs/
// qr_codes.

// Check if the page has been posted to with a product ID.
if (isset($_REQUEST['product_id'])) {

  // Retrieve the product ID.
  $product_id = $_REQUEST['product_id'];
  $product_string = "pid=" . $product_id;

  // Create the data to put into the QR code with the tracking link.
  $qr_link = "http://www.<yoursite>.com/QRscan.php";
  $qr_data .= urlencode($qr_link . "?" . $product_string);

  // Create the full URL for the QR image using Google.
  $qr_generator = "https://chart.googleapis.com/chart?cht=qr";
  $qr_size = "&chs=220x220";
  $qr_data = "&chl=" . $qr_data;
```

```php
    $qr_image = $qr_generator . $qr_size . $qr_data;

} else {

    // Redirect the user if not posted.
    header("Location: QRShareIt.php");
}
?>
```
```html
<!DOCTYPE html>
<html>
<head>
<title>Product Share It Label</title>
<style>
body {
  background: #ddd;
  color: #000;
  font: normal 100%/1.5 tahoma, verdana, sans-serif;
  text-align:center
}
#labelcontainer {
  margin:0 auto;
  background:#fff;
  width:270px;
  padding:20px;
}
fieldset {
  border:5px solid #ccc;
  border-radius: 5px;
  padding: 10px;
}
legend {
  font-size: 1.8em;
  padding: 0 5px;
}
#qrcode {
  position:relative;
}
#prodid {
  font-size:60%;
  text-align:right;
}
</style>
</head>
<body>
  <div id="labelcontainer">
    <fieldset>
      <legend>Scan It. Share It.</legend>
      Like this product? Then scan the QR code below and share it
      with your friends.
      <br/>
      <div id="qrcode">
        <img src="<?php echo $qr_image;?>"/>
```

```
      </div>
      Use our mobile app to scan the code for additional offers.
      <div id="prodid">
        <p><?php echo "PRD-" . $product_id;?></p>
      </div>
    </fieldset>
  </div>
</body>
</html>
```

Figure 5-4 shows the resulting label displayed, showing the QR code image generated from the Google API.

Figure 5-4. Resulting QR code product label

With the "Scan It. Share It." label created, we now need to create the mobile application to scan the QR code and launch the encoded URL. A customer could use one of the many mobile applications available for scanning QR codes, but with a custom mobile application a deeper relationship with your customers can be built. In this part, the RedLaser SDK (*http://redlaser.com/developers/*) will be included in a sample iPhone application to show how easy it is to include QR code scanning in a mobile application.

To use the RedLaser SDK for iOS, download the SDK from here (*http://redlaser.com/developers/*) using the link under "Evaluate for free." If you are implementing an Android solution, RedLaser also provides an SDK for Android API 7 and higher. There is a limit of 25 scans with the evaluation kit; if you wish to include the SDK in a production application, the license pricing is based on a tiered quantity and the number of devices to which your application will be deployed.

The RedLaser SDK for iOS contains a "Using the RedLaser SDK" PDF that provides all the information needed for incorporating the library files (*libRedLaserSDK.a* and *Red LaserSDK.h*) into your project. Also included in the download is a sample iOS project, titled *Sample*. This sample will be the basis for this example and will allow us to quickly create a scanning iOS application.

The sample application provides functionality to scan a code and provide the returned data in a table. For this example the sample will be modified slightly to run the project in your development environment and launch a browser window with the decoded URL. The steps you'll need to take are the following:

1. Replace the Bundle Identifier with your own.
2. Update the `UITableView` of scanned data to allow selection of cells.
3. Add the `didSelectRowAtIndexPath` method for launching the scan selected in a browser on the device.

Open the *RLSample.xcodeproj* file found in the *Sample* directory in your XCode development environment. The minimum version of iOS supported by the RedLaser SDK is iOS 4.0. The first step to get the sample working in your environment is to change the Bundle Identifier of the project to your organization's identifier. By default the identifier of the sample project will be eBay, as seen in Figure 5-5.

Figure 5-5. RLSample bundle identifier

Once you've done this, you should be able to build the project and have it run in device mode on your connected development iPhone.

Next, you'll need to modify the application to allow the user to select the scanned code from the UITableView and have it launch the URL in a browser. By default the sample project will take the scanned data and insert it into a new table cell in a UITableView for viewing purposes. In your own project, you could of course have the browser launched automatically once the code is scanned and confirmed as a valid URL.

To update the UITableView, open the *RLSampleViewController.xib* layout found in the View Controllers → Scan Results Table folder in XCode. By default a view describing the *RLSample* will be displayed on top of the results table. Move this view over a bit to gain access to the UITableView underneath.

Select the UITableView and, in the properties window, change the Selection type from "No Selection" to "Single Selection" (as shown in Figure 5-6). Move the description view back on top of the UITableView.

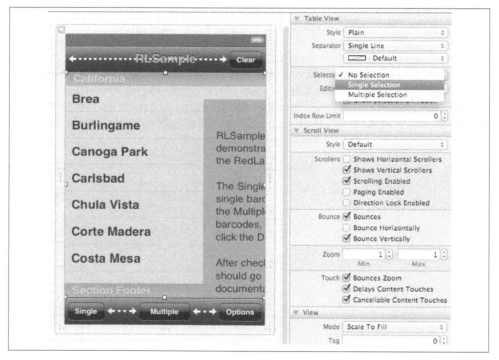

Figure 5-6. Change selection type of table to "Single Selection"

The last step is to have the `RLSampleViewController` launch the device's default browser with the URL scanned from the QR code when a user selects the row in the table of scanned results. Open the *RLSampleViewController.m* file, which is located in the same folder as the *.xib* file. At the end of the method file, add the code in Example 5-3 to catch the row selection event by the user.

Example 5-3. RLSampleViewController.m addition

```
- (void)tableView:(UITableView *)tableView didSelectRowAtIndexPath:
(NSIndexPath *)indexPath {

    // Retrieve cell that has been selected based on indexPath.
    UITableViewCell *cell = [tableView cellForRowAtIndexPath:indexPath];

    // Create URL with the textLabel of the cell, since that is what was
    // scanned.
    NSURL *url = [NSURL URLWithString:cell.textLabel.text];

    // Open the URL that was scanned.
    [[UIApplication sharedApplication] openURL:url];
}
```

Now when the iPhone app is launched on your device you should be able to scan the image of the QR code created earlier, view the link data in the table of results, tap on the table row, and have the URL launched in the browser on your iPhone. The iOS example scanning application is now complete.

To complete the example here, a page for the consumer to land on when the code is scanned by the iOS application needs to be created. The URL encoded in the QR code is set to go to a distribution or "traffic cop" page. There are several benefits to using a distributor configuration instead of going directly to a product landing page. First, if the specific handling of the link needs to change in the future, it will be easier to change the linkage in the traffic handling page, or a database of links behind the scenes, rather than changing the product page. In addition, this will allow for centralized validation of the scanned information and logging of any analytics.

Example 5-4 contains the code for the traffic handler receiving a scanned URL. The traffic handler will validate the product data passed and then forward the session to a specific product-sharing page. Sections have been left as TODOs where you can integrate the code with your specific product and analytics databases.

Example 5-4. QRscan.php

```
<?php
/************************************************************
QRscan.php

Traffic handler for receiving a scanned QR code.
Update stats, and forward appropriately.
```

```
    Called from qr code scan

    **********************************************************/

// Check if the page has been posted to with a product ID.
if (isset($_GET['pid']) && isset($_GET['pky'])) {

    // Retrieve the product ID and product key.
    $product_id = $_GET['pid'];
    $product_key = $_GET['pky'];

    /* Verify that the key is valid by looking in your product
       database.
       TODO: Replace following line with check if key in database
       and guid. */
    $pkeyValid = true;

    if ($pkeyValid) {
      // If valid do the following:

      // 1) Log the scan in your statistics.
      // TODO: Put in your logging functionality.

      // 2) Forward user to the social page with the product guid.
      $sharePage = "SharePage.php?pid=" . $product_id;

      // 3) Forward user to the share page for the product.
      header("Location: " . $sharePage);
    } else {

      // Redirect the user if not from a QR code scan.
      header("Location: InvalidAccess.php");
    }
} else {
    // Redirect the user if not from a QR code scan.
    header("Location: InvalidAccess.php");
}
?>
```

If the data passed in with the URL is correct, the user will be brought to the page for sharing the product with friends via her social network memberships. Example 5-5 shows the code for this page, which will display the links to selected social networks. In your solution, you could have this post on a person's Facebook wall or send an email from a form. This is meant to provide an idea of the possibilities for sharing.

Example 5-5. SharePage.php

```
<?php
/***********************************************************
SharePage.php
```

Allow users to share the specific product with their friends.
Add your own landing page for the product - maybe a central
product support menu for product documentation, email share
with friends, social feed integration, etc.

Call from QRscan.php with the product ID and key.

```
***********************************************************/
?>
<!DOCTYPE html>
<html>
<head>
<title>Share the Product You Love</title>
<meta name="viewport" content="width=device-width; initial-scale=1.0;
  maximum-scale=1.0; user-scalable=0;" />
<style>
body {
  background: #fff;
  color: #000;
  font: normal 100%/1.5 tahoma, verdana, sans-serif;
  text-align:center
}
#container {
  width:270px;
  padding:20px;
}
fieldset {
  border:5px solid #ccc;
  border-radius: 5px;
  padding: 10px;
}
legend {
  font-size: 1.8em;
  padding: 0 5px;
}
</style>
</head>
<body>
  <div id="container">
    <fieldset>
      <legend>Share It.</legend>
      We are glad that you are enjoying your purchase. Share it with
      your friends via your favorite format; email, twitter, facebook,
      google+.
      <br/><br/>
      <img src="images/icn_twitter.png" />
         
      <img src="images/icn_facebook.png" />
      <br/><br/>
      As a thank you after sharing you will be provided a discount
      code off your next purchase.
```

```
      </fieldset>
    </div>
  </body>
</html>
```

Figure 5-7 shows the example product landing page. If a company scanning mobile application is created, you could also launch the sharing page in an embedded `UIWebView` or call web services from the company site to trigger native code and functionality in your application.

Figure 5-7. Landing page on iPhone

In this example, the primary focus has been to provide a simple method for consumers to share a product with friends. However, this same flow and QR code scanning technology could be used to provide product or service support information, coupons, access to detailed product documentation, or a host of other information and services.

See Also

Google Chart Tools: Infographics (QR Codes) (*https://google-developers.appspot.com/chart/infographics/docs/qr_codes*)

RedLaser developer site (*http://redlaser.com/developers/*)

5.2. Creating a Taste Graph

Opportunity

Once a customer has made a purchase from a vendor, there is a window of opportunity to understand the customer's tastes, present him with similar or complementing products, and increase the likelihood of future purchases. The challenge is to present an adequate and applicable set of products that best match the consumer's tastes, also known as a *taste graph*.

Solution

The Hunch.com site contains an ever-growing set of data representing millions of answers to questions by people, product ratings, Facebook likes, venue check-ins, social connections, and user profiles. As commerce developers, all this data provides us with access to a powerful and ever-changing taste graph for the entire Web. Hunch provides an API to access these personalized taste graphs and user trends that we can tap into to make recommendations for our customers.

Discussion

A vendor has a higher potential of making future sales and creating an ongoing relationship with a customer if the vendor can present the customer with personalized product selections. The Hunch API is designed to provide recommendations of movies, books, household products, and more based on data provided about an individual. That data could include anything from a record of products that person has already purchased to her social feed online. Hunch takes this data and, based on millions of other data points, creates a taste graph illustrating the customer's interests.

In addition to the knowledge of any prior purchases, the vendor may have a profile for the customer, which could include that customer's Twitter username. Having the Twitter username is not a requirement to use the Hunch API to provide recommendations, but including the social feed identifier will allow Hunch to personalize the recommendations for the consumer to a much higher level.

 Column Five Media has created an infographic (Hunch Infographic: The Ever Expanding Taste Graph (*http://columnfivemedia.com/work-items/hunch-infographic-the-ever-expanding-taste-graph/*)) that provides just a glimpse of the massive data structure that has been created by Hunch. By comparing users across the Internet, patterns of interests can be formed into highly customized taste graphs for individual consumers. You can go to Hunch.com and try it out with your own free account.

This code example will use two API calls from Hunch to produce product recommendations: `get-results` and `get-recommendations`. Figure 5-8 shows an example of the resulting display of product recommendations for a consumer.

Figure 5-8. Other products presented from Hunch

In our example, the consumer has previously purchased a "KitchenAid Professional 600 series stand mixer" from the vendor and has a Twitter username of *chuckhudson*. With this information, the code will call the Hunch `get-results` API method to retrieve the Hunch ID for the stand mixer product. This is a unique ID for the product that Hunch has assigned; it is prefixed with "hn_", signifying a Hunch ID. In addition, the return from `get-results` will provide a category topic ID for the product, such as "cat_home-garden". Hunch categorizes products into a tree. A product can be included in one or more product topic lists, and each topic list will have a corresponding parent category.

> The full category tree and IDs can be found here (*http://bit.ly/12yBJRS*). If necessary, you can programmatically search and retrieve the topics; for more information see the Hunch API Topic Methods documentation (*http://bit.ly/UPnqE1*).

The Hunch product ID and category topic will be passed into the `get-recommendations` call, along with other data, to determine the best recommendations for the consumer. Both of the calls return JSON strings, and our example code will loop through the results of the `get-recommendations` call and display the images for a set of recommended products. The images will be linked to the appropriate Hunch product pages and each will have a title property set to the item's name, as seen in Figure 5-8.

Example 5-6 shows the code for the *getRecommendations.php* page, which will make the calls to the Hunch API and display the results. The first thing the page will do is to include a library that will be used to sign the calls that are made to the Hunch server and set constants used in the application. To execute API calls against the Hunch server, the application needs to be registered in the Hunch developer environment. To do this, create a developer account and log into the self-service area (*http://hunch.com/develop ers/self-service/signup/*) of the Hunch API developer site. When you've completed your application registration, your application will be assigned an `app_id` and an `app_se cret`. Replace the `app_id` and `app_secret` strings at the top of the *getRecommenda tions.php* file with your application information.

Example 5-6. getRecommendations.php Hunch taste graph recommendations

```
<?
/*************************************************************
getRecommendations.php

Create 3x3 box of recommendations via the Hunch API from a
user's item purchase history and Twitter username taste graph.

*************************************************************/

// Include the auth_sig library.
require_once("libHunchAuthSig.php");

// Define the app constants.
define("HUNCH_API_ROOT","http://api.hunch.com/api/v1");
define("APP_ID","3149331");
define("APP_SECRET","37e05a61369680d9f3605dd899dd455da944e877");

// Define the number of recommendations.
define("LIMIT_NUM",9);

// Function to handle Curl API calls.
function curl_get_file($url) {

  // Initialize the curl request.
  $ch = curl_init();

  // Set the curl options.
  curl_setopt($ch, CURLOPT_AUTOREFERER, TRUE);
  curl_setopt($ch, CURLOPT_FOLLOWLOCATION, TRUE);
  curl_setopt($ch, CURLOPT_HEADER, FALSE);
  curl_setopt($ch, CURLOPT_RETURNTRANSFER, TRUE);
  curl_setopt($ch, CURLOPT_URL, $url);

  // Execute the curl request.
  $data = curl_exec($ch);
  curl_close($ch);
```

```
  return $data;
}

// Function to use the get-results Hunch API call to retrieve the
// Hunch item ID.
function getHunchItemInfo($itemName, $topicList) {

  // Create Hunch URL for get-results call.
  $urlGetRes = HUNCH_API_ROOT."/get-results/?topic_ids=".$topicList.
    "&name=".$itemName."&app_id=".APP_ID;

  // Sign the URL request.
  $urlGetResSigned = signUrl($urlGetRes, APP_SECRET);

  // Make the curl request.
  $strResults = curl_get_file($urlGetResSigned);

  // Convert the JSON results string to an object.
  $objResults = json_decode($strResults);

  // Check the results and set the result_id and topic_id.
  if ($objResults->ok && $objResults->total>0) {
    $result_id = $objResults->results[0]->result_id;
    $topic_id = $objResults->results[0]->topic_ids[0];
  }

  // Return the item result_id and topic_id.
  return array ($result_id, $topic_id);
}

// Function to use get-recommendations to retrieve Hunch
// recommendations.
function getHunchRecommendations($prodName, $listId, $twName) {

  // Get the Hunch item ID and topic category via the get-results API.
  $hunchItemInfo = getHunchItemInfo($prodName, $listId);

  // Set the Hunch item ID and category returned.
  $hnItemId = $hunchItemInfo[0];
  $hnCategory = $hunchItemInfo[1];

  // Modify the Twitter username with the Hunch prefix for Twitter.
  $twName = "tw_".$twName;

  // Construct the get-recommendations API call with the data.
  $urlGetRec = HUNCH_API_ROOT."/get-recommendations/?likes=".$hnItemId.
    "&blocked_result_ids=".$hnItemId."&user_id=".$twName."&topic_ids=".
    $hnCategory."&limit=".LIMIT_NUM."&tags=kitchen&app_id=".APP_ID;

  // Sign the URL request.
  $urlGetRecSigned = signUrl($urlGetRec, APP_SECRET);
```

```php
    // Make the get-recommendations request.
    $strResults = curl_get_file($urlGetRecSigned);

    return $strResults;
}
?>
```

```html
<!DOCTYPE html>
<html>
<head>
<title>Recommendations</title>
<style>
body {color: #000; font: normal 100%/1.5 tahoma, verdana, sans-serif;
  text-align: center}
#reccontainer {margin: 0 auto; background: #fff; width: 340px;
  padding:20px;}
fieldset {border: 2px solid #ccc; border-radius: 5px; padding: 10px;}
legend {font-size: 1em; padding: 0 5px;}
.productHolder {float: left; width: 100px; height: 100px;}
.productImage {max-width: 100px; max-height: 100px;}
</style>
</head>
<body>
  <div id="reccontainer">
    <fieldset>
      <legend>Other Product Ideas</legend>
```

```php
<?php
        // Set the item recently purchased, Hunch list topic,
        // and Twitter username.
        $itemName = "kitchenaid-professional-600-series-stand-mixer-
          kp26m1xnp";
        $hunchList = "list_electric-mixer";
        $twitterUsername = "chuckhudson";

        // Make function call to get the recommendations.
        $strRecommendations = getHunchRecommendations($itemName,
          $hunchList,$twitterUsername);

        // Convert the recommendations JSON string to an object.
        $objRecs = json_decode($strRecommendations);

        // Check the results to verify success.
        if ($objRecs->ok && $objRecs->total>0) {

            // Loop through each recommendation and display linked image.
            foreach($objRecs->recommendations as $recommendation) {
              echo '<div class="productHolder">';
              echo '<a href="'.$recommendation->url.'"
                      title="'.$recommendation->title.'">';
              echo '<img class="productImage"
                        src="'.$recommendation->image_url.'" />';
              echo '</a>';
```

```
      echo '</div>';
    }
  } else {
    echo "No Recommendations Found.";
  }
?>

    </fieldset>
  </div>
</body>
</html>
```

As mentioned earlier, each request to the Hunch API should be signed and referenced to the application registered. The `app_id` associated with the application will be included as a query string parameter for the API call, while the `app_secret` will be passed into the authentication signature function in the *libHunchAuthsig.php* file to create a unique signature for the call request.

 The Hunch API has a quota per registered application of 5,000 calls per day. If you find that you need a higher quota, you can contact support at Hunch.com (*api@hunch.com*).

Hunch provides a library helper function to hash the URL and create the `auth_sig`, listed in Example 5-7. The core function of the helper file is `signUrl`; it takes the string URL of the API call and the application's secret key. The function organizes the query string parameters and creates a unique encoded signature held in a query string variable named `auth_sig`. The `auth_sig` is appended to the URL and returned from the function. The URL request is now valid with the `auth_sig` token and can be sent to the Hunch servers via the `curl_get_file` function.

Example 5-7. libHunchAuthSig.php Hunch request signing

```php
<?php
/************************************************************
libHunchAuthSig.php

Library to sign a Hunch API call based on an app_secret.

Source of file:
http://hunch.com/developers/v1/resources/samples/#signing


************************************************************/

// Helper function to the signUrl function.
function enc($c) {
  $c = str_replace(array('+', '/', '@', '%20'), array('%2B', '%2F',
      '%40', '+'), $c);
  return $c;
```

```
}

// Function to create the signed URL from the URL and secret_key
// (app_secret) passed in.
function signUrl($url, $secret_key)
{
  $original_url = $url;
  $urlparts = parse_url($url);

  // Build $params with each name/value pair.
  foreach (split('&', $urlparts['query']) as $part) {
    if (strpos($part, '=')) {
      list($name, $value) = split('=', $part, 2);
    } else {
      $name = $part;
      $value = '';
    }
    $params[$name] = $value;
  }

  // Sort the array by key.
  ksort($params);

  // Build the canonical query string.
  $canonical = '';
  foreach ($params as $key => $val) {
    $canonical .= "$key=".enc(utf8_encode($val))."&";
  }

  // Remove the trailing ampersand.
  $canonical = preg_replace("/&$/", '', $canonical);

  // Build the sign.
  $string_to_sign = enc($canonical) . $secret_key;

  // Calculate our actual signature and base64-encode it.
  $signature = bin2hex(hash('sha1', $string_to_sign, $secret_key));

  // Finally, rebuild the URL with the proper string and include the
  // signature.
  $url = "{$urlparts['scheme']}://{$urlparts['host']}
    {$urlparts['path']}?$canonical&auth_sig=".rawurlencode($signature);
  return $url;
}
?>
```

The following URL request shows the `get-results` request for this example prior to the addition of the `auth_sig` token from signing the URL. The topic ID and product name to search for have been included:

> *http://api.hunch.com/api/v1/get-results/?topic_ids=list_electric-*
> *mixer&name=kitchenaid-professional-600-series-stand-mixer-kp26m1xnp*

Once the get-results call is made, a JSON string is returned from Hunch, as displayed in Figure 5-9. In this case one item has been returned from the Hunch taste graph, as defined in the total property. The ok property value of true informs the code that the Hunch API executed the call successfully.

```
{
    total: 1,
    ok: true,
  - results: [
      - {
            preferences: [ ],
          + rating_counts: { ... },
            description: "Designed with all-metal construction and a 6-quart capacity, this powerful stand mix
          - topic_ids: [
                "cat_home-garden",
                "list_electric-mixer"
            ],
            url: "http://hunch.com/item/hn_244581/kitchenaid-professional-600-series-stand-mixer-kp26m1xnp/",
            price: 367.49,
            title: "KitchenAid Professional 600 Series Stand Mixer - KP26M1XNP",
          + image_urls: [ ... ],
            image_url: "http://aka-img-1.h-img.com/media/img/b/hn/244581/4660575413148900578",
          + lists: { ... },
          + urls: [ ... ],
            affiliate_links: [ ],
          + aliases: [ ... ],
            result_id: "hn_244581",
          + average_ratings: { ... },
          - tags: [
                "cooking",
                "kitchen appliance",
                "countertop",
                "electric mixer",
                "bread dough"
            ],
            name: "KitchenAid Professional 600 Series Stand Mixer - KP26M1XNP"
        }
    ],
  + warnings: [ ... ]
}
```

Figure 5-9. Hunch get-results JSON results

The first property that we will retrieve is the result_id, which corresponds to the Hunch unique product ID.

 To quickly validate the Hunch result_id for an item, you can load the following URL in a browser window, replacing the "hn_" number used here with the Hunch ID for the item: *http://hunch.com/item/ hn_244011*. If successful, the item product page will be viewable in the browser.

The second property returned is the first topic_id element, which in this case is "cat_home-garden". This is the parent category for the item in the Hunch category tree; you can pass it into the get-recommendations call to limit the results to only this category.

Once the product ID and category topic ID are retrieved from the get-results call, the get-recommendations request can be constructed. The get-recommendations parameters are a bit more complicated: they consist of variables that allow the Hunch API to narrow down the taste graph of product recommendations to be created. The `re sult_id` that was retrieved from the `get-results` call is used in two ways in the new request: to tell Hunch what the person likes already via a `likes` query string variable (providing the Hunch graph with a starting point), and to instruct Hunch to not present this product in the results, since the consumer has already purchased the product, via the `blocked_result_ids` query string parameter.

Next, the request contains other data points by which the taste graph can be honed: the `user_id` and `topic_ids`. The `user_id` represents a social stream for the consumer, referencing the consumer's Twitter username. To tell Hunch that this is a Twitter username, the username is prefixed with the characters "tw_". The list of prefixes and services integrated into Hunch are available on the Hunch developer site; they include social network systems such as Facebook and Twitter. The `topic_ids` correlate to topic IDs from the Hunch category tree. In this case the topic ID "cat_home-garden" will be used to limit the results to those products in the home and garden space:

> http://api.hunch.com/api/v1/get-recommendations/?
> likes=hn_244581&blocked_result_ids=hn_244581&user_id=tw_chuckhudson&
> topic_ids=cat_home-garden&limit=9&tags=kitchen

The final two query string variables are `limit` and `tags`. The `limit` element with a value of 9 tells Hunch to only return a maximum of nine recommendations. If this element is not included, by default Hunch will return 10 recommendations; however, we only need 9 products to fill our 3 × 3 recommendations grid. The final element, `tags`, contains any special tags that we want the recommended products to contain. Each product in the Hunch system can have keyword tags associated with it. If you refer back to Figure 5-9, you'll see the `tags` value with a set of tags corresponding to the product returned. In this example, a tag value of "kitchen" will be included in the `get- recommendations` request to limit the results to just those products that have a "kitchen" tag.

The JSON response from the `get-recommendations` call, shown in Figure 5-10, contains an ok status flag showing that the call was successful and a `total` value of 73, showing the total number of recommendations found for the request. Only nine products are returned, though, because the `limit` tag was included in the request.

At the root of the JSON response is a variable called `is_personalized`, which can be either `true` or `false`. A `true` value for this variable informs us that Hunch was able to personalize the results to the user based on knowledge of the user in the Hunch data structure. This is where the Twitter username becomes useful—without the `user_id` the results would only have been based on a collective knowledge of other people's "like" of the product.

```
{
+ warnings: [ .. ],
  total: 73,
  ok: true,
  is_personalized: true,
- recommendations: [
    - {
        + average_ratings: { .. },
        + rating_counts: { .. },
          stars: 5,
          wildcard: false,
        + topic_ids: [ .. ],
        + image_urls: [ .. ],
          lists: { },
          is_personalized: true,
          is_predicted: true,
          name: "Han Solo in Carbonite Ice Cube Tray",
          preferences: [ ],
          title: "Han Solo in Carbonite Ice Cube Tray",
          url: "http://hunch.com/item/hn_4050401/han-solo-in-carbonite-ice-cube-tray/",
        + tags: [ .. ],
          is_saved: false,
          popularity: 0,
        + score: [ .. ],
          image_url: "http://aka-img-1.h-img.com/media/img/b/hn/4050401/998493543484608010",
        + urls: [ .. ],
          affiliate_links: [ ],
        + aliases: [ .. ],
          result_id: "hn_4050401"
      },
    + { .. },
    + { .. },
    + { .. },
    + { .. },
    + { .. },
    + { .. },
    + { .. },
    + { .. },
    + { .. }
  ]
}
```

Figure 5-10. Hunch get-recommendations JSON results

Packaged in the `get-recommendations` response is an array of the recommendations
returned under the `recommendations` element. In each recommendation are several
properties, including the title, the image URL address, and a URL to the listing for the
product or service on Hunch. As well, each recommendation contains a unique `re
sult_id`, which is the unique ID for the product or service. In this example the code
will loop through each recommendation and pull out the image URL, Hunch URL, and
title to display in our recommendations box. In your implementation, the Hunch IDs
could be tied to the products in your product catalogue instead of using the Hunch
product links.

 In this example the Hunch API calls were made one after another, with
the second call using results from the first. Hunch has a special API in
addition to the results-oriented API that contains a "batch" call for
making multiple calls in one request. You can explore this call in the
online Hunch API Special Methods documentation (*http://hunch.com/
developers/v1/docs/reference/#special-methods*).

See Also

Hunch Developer Area (*http://hunch.com/developers/v1/*)

Hunch API Reference (*http://hunch.com/developers/v1/docs/reference/*)

Hunch API Reference – Result Methods (*http://hunch.com/developers/v1/docs/refer ence/#result-methods*)

Hunch API Console (*http://hunch.com/developers/v1/resources/console*)

Hunch API Topics (*http://hunch.com/developers/v1/resources/topics/*)

5.3. Social Recommendations

Opportunity

Social recommendations can be a powerful driver of future sales, often leading to new revolutions of the commerce lifecycle. Most of the time social recommendations come from customers sharing their interests and things they like with people in their social circles. Technically, to make recommendations ourselves we have had to perform multiple and potentially exponentially growing numbers of web service calls. If a data retrieval and aggregation gateway could be available to call services such as Hunch and eBay, providing mashups of social recommendations to visitors could be easier and more straightforward.

Solution

Fortunately, we're not the first to face the challenge of mashing together large sets of data from multiple services around the Web. In fact, the platform engineers at eBay have created an open source system called *ql.io* that can, from a single request, perform calls to multiple web services with access to large data sets, join the relational data, and return the result set in various formats. This is an overly simple definition of the power of ql.io, but it will suffice for our needs. For this example, we will make a single request from client-side JavaScript to a ql.io URL that will return a list of recommendations from eBay mashed together based on recommendations from the Hunch services, as seen in the previous example in this chapter. Using ql.io will make this mashup quite simple, reducing the amount of data transmitted and the processing required to display the information.

Discussion

For this mashup, we will allow the viewer to input a friend's Twitter username into a form, select a category, and have a set of recommended items from eBay in a specific category presented. The items presented will contain a picture (if available), a title, and a link to the item on the eBay site for bidding or purchase. Through the eBay Finding API, eBay provides a `findItemsByKeywords` call that will return a list of items (and their details) that match a set of search criteria. The search criteria used in the request will include keywords. To get the keywords to search against with the eBay call, we'll again use the Hunch `get-recommendations` call that we used in the last example (Recipe 5.2, "Creating a Taste Graph"). This will allow us to retrieve a list of keywords based on a Twitter username. To merge the results of the two services, multiple calls would normally need to be made in a specific order, culling the data from one result to be used in the request of the next call. This is where the power of ql.io shines through.

The ql.io service provides the framework for creating multirelational models from multiple APIs. The ql.io architecture reuses key technology concepts, such as SQL and JSON, to provide the developer with tools to build new models that can be accessed in a single API request. The new models and requests can be employed on the ql.io system in a remotely hosted data model, or on your own system.

The ql.io domain servers should only be used for your own development and testing of calls, as they are not set up to serve as a scalable production system. By default ql.io servers have timeouts in place to protect the requests of multiple developers. To create your own ql.io app instance and service, you will need the Node platform; follow the instructions for installing a ql.io app (*http://ql.io/docs/build-an-app*).

The ql.io system is an open source project available on GitHub (*https://github.com/ql-io/ql.io*) and released under the Apache License, version 2.0.

The basic concept of ql.io is that you can call an API service and a table of the results can be created. When you have one or more of these tables, you can write a sub-`select` to retrieve mashed-up data in one call. There are two steps to extrapolating and creating your own ql.io mashup of data:

1. Create the data model tables from the API call results.
2. Write the `selects` and `joins` to relate the data together.

An excellent quick-start tutorial that demonstrates these steps is available here (*http://ql.io/docs/quickstart*). By default the ql.io online system includes several predefined tables based on the APIs of services such as Bing, Bitly, eBay, Google, and Twitter. To see which tables are predefined in ql.io, run the following query using the *show tables* command:

http://ql.io/q=s?showtables

Figure 5-11 shows the JSON results block, which includes the `table` name, `about` command, and `info` string of each table.

```
[
    - {
        name:  "eBay.ProductReviews",
        about:  "/table?name=eBay.ProductReviews",
        info:  "<p>eBay <a href="http://developer.ebay.com/devzone
    },
    - {
        name:  "ebay.SellingManagerInventoryFolder",
        about:  "/table?name=ebay.SellingManagerInventoryFolder",
        info:  ""
    },
    - {
        name:  "ebay.getallbidders",
        about:  "/table?name=ebay.getallbidders",
        info:  "<p>eBay <a href="http://developer.ebay.com/devzone
    },
    - {
        name:  "google.geocode",
        about:  "/table?name=google.geocode",
        info:  "<p>Google geocoding and shopping APIs</p>"
    },
```

Figure 5-11. ql.io show tables result

To view the information on a specific table, use the table ql.io service with the name of the table. For example, to get the details of the `ebay.finditems` table, you would use the following URL:

http://ql.io/table?name=finditems

The resulting page will show how the table is constructed using a URI template and `GET` method. ql.io uses the URI template to replace fields in the URIs with dynamic variables (marked with curly braces).

 The ql.io tables (*http://ql.io/tables*) and routes (*http://ql.io/api*) can also be found online.

ql.io already has the `finditems` table for eBay created, so we won't need to create this table. The documentation on the `finditems` table reveals that there are a number of parameters available, with only one required: `keywords`. The value of the `keywords` parameter will be a list of the titles of the recommendations that are returned from the `get-recommendations` call to Hunch. However, there is no Hunch `get-recommendations` table by default in ql.io, so we will need to create this table.

To create a table, ql.io uses the SQL `create` command based on the results of a `select` `get` command. The Hunch table `create` command for ql.io will be:

```
create table hunch on select get from "http://api.hunch.com/api/v1/get-
recommendations/?user_id={uid}&topic_id={tid}&limit={limit}" using
defaults limit="10" resultset "recommendations";
```

Notice that the `create` command creates a table from the results of the same call we used in Recipe 5.2, "Creating a Taste Graph" by calling the `get-recommendations` API method with a user ID, a topic ID, and a limit. The resulting table will be titled "hunch," and the call will use the default of 10 for the number of recommendations to return (the `limit`). The three parameters are passed using a URI template containing variables.

Now that we have a command to create the table for the Hunch recommendations and a default table definition in ql.io for the eBay `finditems` table, we can put the two together with a SQL `select` statement:

```
select * from finditems where keywords in (select title from hunch
where uid="tw_chuckhudson" and tid="cat_electronics")
```

The SQL `select` is the trigger for making all the calls for filling the tables and creating a result set of data. Here, the `uid` and `tid`, or user ID and topic ID, are being passed into the Hunch table defined earlier. The results from the table call are then passed into the eBay `finditems` `keywords` parameter. The result is a blend of multiple calls from two different APIs. In practice, this is a simple example of using ql.io; the number of tables and `select`s could grow quite large depending on your specific use case, but hopefully the methodology for creating a relational data model from large data stores using ql.io is clear.

To test whether the tables and `select`s are defined correctly, ql.io provides a convenient HTTP interface that you can access by opening a browser and pasting in your URL-encoded script. To do this, use a URL of the form:

http://ql.io/q?s={url-encoded script}

Or, for a JSON-P implementation with a callback method, use:

http://ql.io/q?s={url-encoded script}&callback={func}

So, to test the script for this example with the table creation and `select` statements, you can paste the test URL in Example 5-9 into your browser's address bar (a decoded version of the script has been included in Example 5-8 for easier reading, but for testing purposes you'll need to use the URL-encoded version in Example 5-9).

Example 5-8. ql.io test URL (decoded)

```
http://ql.io/q?s=create table hunch on select get from "http://api.hunch.com/api/v1/
get-recommendations/?user_id={uid}&topic_id={tid}&limit={limit}" using
defaults limit="10" resultset "recommendations";select * from finditems
where keywords in (select title from hunch where uid="tw_chuckhudson"
and tid="cat_electronics")
```

Example 5-9. ql.io test URL (encoded)

```
http://ql.io/q?s=create%20table%20hunch%20on%20select%20get%20from%20%
22http%3A%2F%2Fapi.hunch.com%2Fapi%2Fv1%2Fget-recommendations%2F%
3Fuser_id%3D%7Buid%7D%26topic_id%3D%7Btid%7D%26limit%3D%7Blimit%7D%22%
20using%20defaults%20limit%3D%2210%22%20resultset%20%22recommendations%
22%3B%0A%0Aselect%20*%20from%20finditems%20where%20keywords%20in%
20(select%20title%20from%20hunch%20where%20uid%3D%22tw_chuckhudson%22%
20and%20tid%3D%22cat_electronics%22)
```

The ql.io servers will take the HTTP request, create the Hunch table, perform the subsequent API requests, mash up the results into a JSON block, and return the block to the browser, as shown in Figure 5-12.

```
[
  - {
      itemId: "221123205905",
      title: "Brand New BEDPHONES Sleep Sound Headphones - Designed for Sleep",
      globalId: "EBAY-US",
    - primaryCategory: {
        categoryId: "112529",
        categoryName: "Headphones"
      },
      galleryURL: "http://thumbs2.ebaystatic.com/m/mvLQLWpJanFHvbLaD9c7hNQ/140.
      viewItemURL: "http://www.ebay.com/itm/Brand-New-BEDPHONES-Sleep-Sound-Head
      paymentMethod: "PayPal",
      autoPay: "true",
      postalCode: "64119",
      location: "Kansas City,MO,USA",
      country: "US",
    + sellerInfo: { ... },
    + shippingInfo: { ... },
    + sellingStatus: { ... },
    + listingInfo: { ... },
      returnsAccepted: "false",
    + condition: { ... },
      isMultiVariationListing: "false"
    },
  + { ... },
  + { ... },
  + { ... },
```

Figure 5-12. JSON eBay items returned from ql.io

Now that the ql.io call has been defined, the call can be used in either server-side or client-side programming. In this case the call will be used via client-side scripting with JQuery, as in Example 5-10, to make the remote call based on the user inputting a Twitter username and selecting a category (the categories are from the Hunch topic tree, as discussed in the previous example). You could make the call in PHP, as shown in the previous example with Hunch, but this shows pushing the overhead to the client browser. Once the user submits the form, the ql.io request will be dynamically created and made (using the JQuery getJSON method) to the ql.io endpoint to retrieve the eBay items.

Example 5-10. qlSocialRec.html social recommendations

```
<!DOCTYPE html>
<html>
<head>
<meta charset="UTF-8" />
<title>eBay Recommendations</title>
<style>
body {color: #000; font: normal 100%/1.5 tahoma, verdana, sans-serif;}
.itemImage {max-width: 75px; max-height: 75px;}
.itemrow {position: relative; clear: both; width: 500px;
  height: 80px; border: 1px solid #ccc;}
.gallery {position: relative; float: left; width: 80px; height: 80px;
  border: 1px solid #ccc;}
.info {position: relative; float: right; text-overflow: ellipsis;
  overflow: hidden; white-space: nowrap; width: 416px;
  height: 80px; border: 1px solid #ccc;}
legend {font-size: 1.3em; padding-left: 5px; padding-right: 5px;
  position: relative;}
fieldset {border: 1px solid #ccc; border-radius: 5px; float: left;
  paddng: 10px; width: 520px;}
li {clear: both; list-style-type: none; margin: 0 0 10px;}
label, input, select {font-size: 1.0em;}
label {width: 200px}
input {border: 2px solid #ccc; border-radius: 5px;
  padding: 5px 25px 5px 5px; width: 285px;}
</style>
<script src="http://code.jquery.com/jquery-latest.js"></script>
<script>

// Function to initialize any page handlers.
function init() {
  // Set up the button click handler.
  var btnSubmit = document.getElementById('btnSubmit');
  btnSubmit.addEventListener('click',getSocialRecs,false);
}

// Function to get the recommendations from ql.io.
function getSocialRecs() {

  // Clear the current list of eBay items.
  document.getElementById("items").innerHTML = "";

  // Retrieve the form fields.
  var uid = document.getElementById('uid').value;
  var tid = document.getElementById('tid').value;

  // Construct the URL for JSON retrieval from ql.io.
  var jsonUrl = 'http://ql.io/q?s=';
  var qTblCreate = 'create table hunch on select get from
    "http://api.hunch.com/api/v1/get-
    recommendations/?user_id={uid}&topic_id={tid}&limit={limit}"
    using defaults limit="10" resultset "recommendations";';
```

```
    var qSelect = 'select * from finditems where keywords in (select
      title from hunch where uid="'+uid+'" and tid="'+tid+'")';

    var getUrl = jsonUrl + encodeURIComponent(qTblCreate + qSelect) +
      "&callback=?";

    // Execute the JQuery call to ql.io.
    $.getJSON(getUrl,
      function(data) {
        // Loop through each item returned and display.
        $.each(data, function(i,item){
          displayItem(item);
        });
    });
}

// Display helper to display each eBay item.
function displayItem(item) {
  var outputHTML = "";

  outputHTML += '<div class="itemrow">';
  outputHTML += '<div class="gallery"><img src="'+item.galleryURL+'"
    class="itemImage"/></div>';
  outputHTML += '<div class="info"><a
    href="'+item.viewItemURL+'">'+item.title+'</a></div>';
  outputHTML += '</div>';

  var divItems = document.getElementById("items");
  divItems.innerHTML += outputHTML;
}

// Call the init function on page load.
window.addEventListener('load',init,false);

</script>
</head>
<body>
  <div id="socRecForm">
    <fieldset>
      <legend>Retrieve eBay Recommendations</legend>
      <ol>
        <li>
          <label for="username">
            Twitter or Facebook Username (tw_ or fb_)
          </label>
          <input type="text" id="uid" value="tw_chuckhudson" /><br/>
        </li>
      </ol>
      <ol>
        <li>
          <label for="topic">Hunch Category</label>
          <select id="tid">
```

```
            <option value="cat_art-design">Art & design</option>
            <option value="cat_electronics">Electronics</option>
            <option value="cat_health">Health</option>
            <option value="cat_home-garden">Home & Garden</option>
          </select>
        </li>
      </ol>
      <button id="btnSubmit">Submit</button>
    </fieldset>
  </div>
  <div id="items"></div>
</body>
</html>
```

If you deploy your own ql.io app, you can preload the `create table` and `select` statements so that a call can be aliased to a route using the `get` method. This will allow you to then make a call to your own route, which exposes your API. Information on how to add your own route in the ql.io `select` can be found in the ql.io "Build an App Locally" (*http://ql.io/docs/build-an-app*) documentation.

The results from running Example 5-10 can be seen in Figure 5-13. Note that the Twitter or Facebook username will need to be entered, with the initials of the specific service added to the beginning of the username.

The power of ql.io can be demonstrated by running the example script here in the test console (*http://ql.io/console*) that ql.io provides. In the console, add your ql.io script and click "run."

Figure 5-14 shows how just asking for recommendations of eBay items results in 11 separate calls to Hunch and eBay. The Hunch API request returns 10 titles of recommendations, which are then each sent to eBay in subsequent and separate calls to find the resulting items. ql.io then merges the results, as shown in Figure 5-15, and returns the results in JSON.

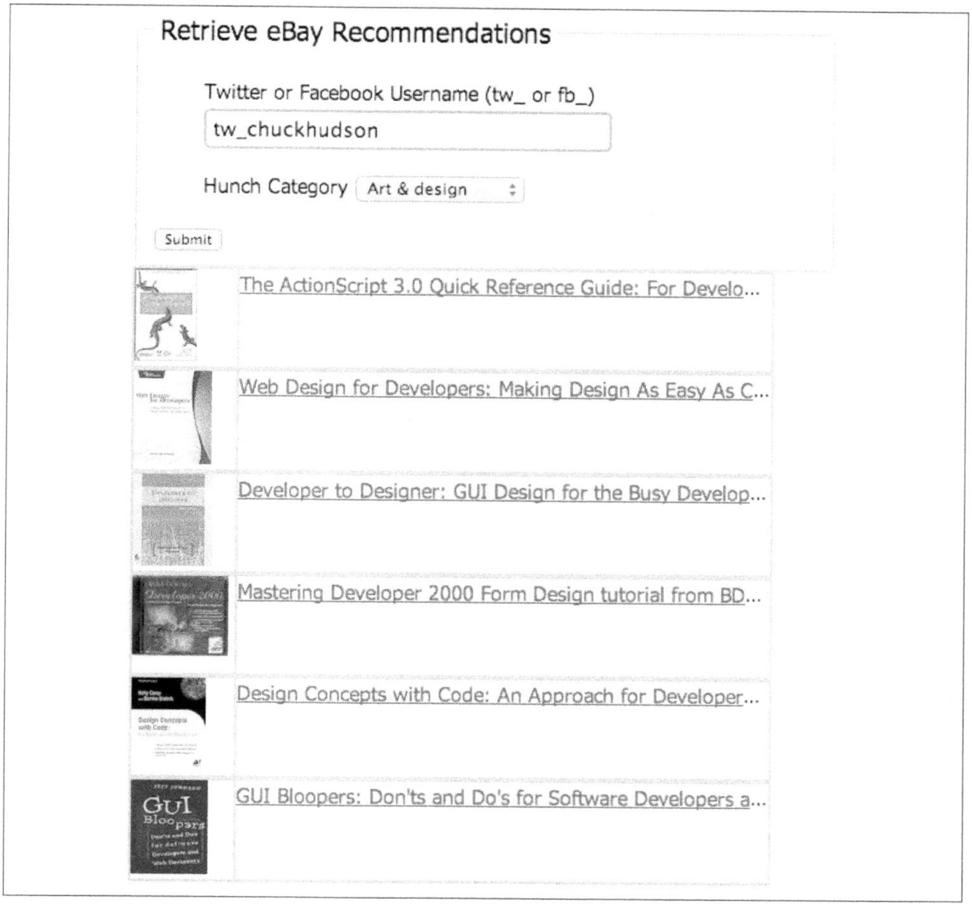

Figure 5-13. eBay item results from Hunch mashup

When developing commerce applications, there are times when it is necessary to programmatically create mashups of data from your own data and external data stores. In this example, we have explored how to leverage ql.io's relational modeling of large data sets to provide targeted social recommendations. The example here has been relatively simple, and the ql.io framework can be leveraged to mash up many more large sets of data, and in different ways. The intent of this example was to show the capability and means of displaying targeted and succinct social recommendations given user-provided information. If done well and positioned with customers, this information can cue another round of the commerce lifecycle.

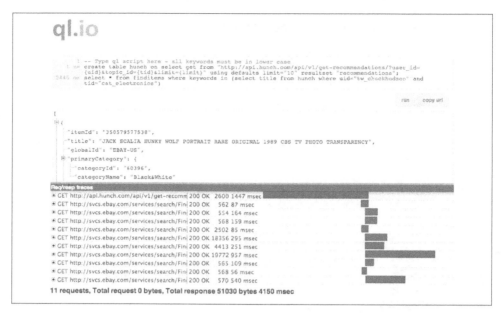

Figure 5-14. Output from ql.io console

See Also

About ql.io (*http://ql.io/docs/about*)

ql.io Quick Start (*http://ql.io/docs/quickstart*)

ql.io HTTP Interface (*http://ql.io/docs/http*)

Hunch API Reference – get-recommendations (*http://hunch.com/developers/v1/docs/reference/#result-methods*)

eBay Finding API Call Reference (*http://developer.ebay.com/devzone/finding/callref/finditemsbykeywords.html*)

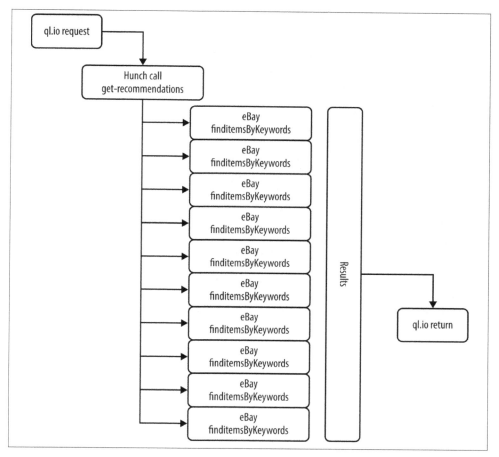

Figure 5-15. Call flow for ql.io social recommendations

5.4. Conclusion

In many cases, after the sale and fulfillment stages the commerce lifecycle ends for a vendor. However, there is an opportunity to feed the lifecycle again, by making targeted product recommendations, or making it easy for customers to make recommendations to their social contacts based on their happiness with the products or services that you sell. As the saying goes, "the best future customer is the customer you have already," and the costs of acquiring new customers can be considerable. By incorporating available APIs, you can not only create long-lasting relationships with your present customers but also leverage their help to lower customer acquisition costs by spreading the word about your products and services through their social circles.

In this chapter we have looked at a few examples, including the use of QR codes with the RedLaser SDK to streamline the flow for customers to share product information with people in their social circles. Using this technology, customers can easily and quickly share products with their online social networks via their smartphones. There are many other uses for QR codes, but this example shows the benefit of connecting QR codes with social networking to drive commerce.

The second example in this chapter leveraged the Hunch API to make smart recommendations based on a person's online social postings. This can be integrated into your web or mobile application in multiple ways; for example, providing recommendations for a present customer or creating a tool for suggesting products for another given person. Building upon the second example, the last exercise leveraged the ql.io service with Hunch and eBay to build a mashup of targeted products on eBay for a given Twitter user. This example showed two key benefits to using ql.io in this manner: mashing up the results of multiple API calls from across the Web, and creating a set of targeted recommendations using online social network user information.

Ultimately, incorporating the examples in this chapter along with the APIs discussed to make sharing of product information easy and social recommendations more targeted will prime new revolutions of the commerce lifecycle.

About the Author

Chuck Hudson has been at the intersection of web business and technology since the inception of online commerce in the mid 1990s. Having programmed in numerous web and mobile languages, he combines a passion for the commerce lifecycle and a wealth of experience to create innovative solutions. He is currently a Director of Application Development focusing on HTML5, iOS, and Android products. With an MBA focused on entrepreneurship and managing technologically innovative enterprises, Chuck has been a successful entrepreneur and consulted with multiple companies on web and mobile product and service strategies. He shares his knowledge of web and mobile product execution through business advisory roles and as a visiting faculty member in the Masters of Internet Technology program at the Terry College of Business, University of Georgia. Chuck has spoken and led lab sessions on web and mobile best practices at development conferences nationally and internationally. In 2008, he received the eBay Star Developer award for the first iOS-based web and native applications for users of eBay. Chuck is also a certified PayPal developer and certified PHP programmer, and sits on the PayPal Developers Council.

Have it your way.

Get even more for your money.

Join the O'Reilly Community, and register the O'Reilly books you own. It's free, and you'll get:

- $4.99 ebook upgrade offer
- 40% upgrade offer on O'Reilly print books
- Membership discounts on books and events
- Free lifetime updates to ebooks and videos
- Multiple ebook formats, DRM FREE
- Participation in the O'Reilly community
- Newsletters
- Account management
- 100% Satisfaction Guarantee

Signing up is easy:

1. **Go to: oreilly.com/go/register**
2. **Create an O'Reilly login.**
3. **Provide your address.**
4. **Register your books.**

Note: English-language books only

To order books online:
oreilly.com/store

For questions about products or an order:
orders@oreilly.com

To sign up to get topic-specific email announcements and/or news about upcoming books, conferences, special offers, and new technologies:
elists@oreilly.com

For technical questions about book content:
booktech@oreilly.com

To submit new book proposals to our editors:
proposals@oreilly.com

O'Reilly books are available in multiple DRM-free ebook formats. For more information:
oreilly.com/ebooks

O'REILLY®

Spreading the knowledge of innovators   oreilly.com

Ingram Content Group UK Ltd.
Milton Keynes UK
UKHW031909160323
418699UK00014B/365